A First Step into
a Much Larger World

A First Step into
a Much Larger World

The Christian University and Beyond

JOHN W. HAWTHORNE

WIPF & STOCK · Eugene, Oregon

A FIRST STEP INTO A MUCH LARGER WORLD
The Christian University and Beyond

Wipf & Stock
An Imprint of Wipf and Stock Publishers
199 W. 8th Ave., Suite 3
Eugene, OR 97401

www.wipfandstock.com

ISBN 13: 978-1-62032-947-4

Manufactured in the U.S.A.

For Rosa Pavlova Hawthorne

*May you find your place in the world
while changing it for the better.*

Contents

Foreword

Without a doubt, our world is experiencing change at a greater pace than ever. However, there is one thing that must not change— the dynamic, enriching educational experience of a Christian college or university.

When thinking of their mission, Christian colleges and universities need to wrestle with an introspective question – are we pursuing excellence in all areas of the educational experience we offer to our students [and their future]? This is why I am so interested in this book and its call to deeper and richer conversations—among and between faculty, students, staff, and administrators.

Such an institution provides an educational context that not only prepares students with qualities such as ethics, integrity, the ability to think critically and analytically and to communicate effectively, but it prepares students for life itself. Such an education does not focus on achieving narrow academic requirements or professional certifications, but on the total development of each student. An education infused and shaped by Christian thought should provide a sense of wholeness, solidity, and focus for students in the midst of an ever-changing economic and social landscape.

Since the time I was an undergraduate, the issues and life challenges facing college students seem to have multiplied and become increasingly complex. Given this, as the president of a Christian university and as a parent, I am deeply interested in the foundational values and life direction that greatly influence college students. Although attending a Christian college or university does not guarantee that a student's decisions and choices will align with God's intentions for their life, it does provide an environment, community, and shaping philosophy that is designed to place such considerations before them.

Such a university should be a place of conversation about the beautiful, just, courageous, and wise; a place that fosters transformation by joining hope, faith, and love as a witness to the truth. It is a construct and application that forms a balanced, holistic student experience.

Unfortunately, some institutions become imbalanced in their focus, priorities, and attention to the life of faith and the mind. It is imperative that academic excellence and intellectual development be the primary pursuit for a Christian college and university. Colossians 3:17, "Whatever you do, whether in word or deed, do it all in the name of the Lord Jesus, giving thanks to God the Father through him."

A faculty colleague reminded me recently that there exists a special ethical duty for Christian colleges and universities to deliver an educational experience that will not simply nurture a student's faith and prepare them for life, but offer one that will foster the height and breadth of their potential for a thriving and meaningful life. It isn't a contractual relationship with students, but one that is covenantal—it is promise-oriented rather than an if/then proposition. Given this, it is imperative for colleges and universities to determine what they are promising students (and, question whether it is enough) and then deliver that promise—for their sake, and for the sake of our world.

Living a balanced life will position one to follow God's call for expanded influence and transformational impact through a life called into being **by** Him and **for** Him. The message of balance is found in the call to become like Christ. As the recipients of grace and mercy, we are compelled to engage the world in the same manner in which God did in Christ, that is, through incarnational love. Being restored in His image enables us to reflect God's love. As we do, we become the living embodiments of God's love, a redemptive presence in the world.

As God is in the process of reconciling the world and making it right, he uses us to be his hands and feet in the process—called to be people who set the world right: bringing justice to orphans and widows, hope to the lost, sight to the blind, and freedom to those who are held captive.

Those of us who follow Christ are called to be a People of Promise. We are descendants of Abram, and share in the inheritance promised to him by God in Genesis 12. It is interesting that Abram didn't know where he was going, but he knew his **purpose**. They were to be a People of Promise. It was God's desire to bless the world through Abram and his people. God was calling them to the Promised Land—to a purpose, and to a vision.

The promise to bless the world through Abram didn't end with Abram. The promise and the call have been passed down through generation to generation, from Abram, to Isaac, to Jacob, to Joseph, to Moses, to Joshua and on to us today. It is our generation's time to carry the vision forward and Christian colleges and universities should be primary generators to perpetuate this call—to challenge students with discovering their purpose in life.

In this book, Dr. John Hawthorne invites us into a conversation. Each participant in the educational process should fully engage in the experience. My hope is that Christian higher education would be a place of open and honest conversation, seeking truth in all areas of life. There is both an institutional aspect to this hope as well as an individual one.

For institutions, it is my hope that excellence would be pursued, in all ways and in all areas. Pursuing the highest standard will fulfill our responsibility to our students for their own professional development and future. Beyond this, fully engaging in developing the whole person with the vision to carry forward the idea of being a people of promise will challenge students to think of life beyond and to be leaven in their communities.

John Wesley used the metaphor of a mirror—we are called not only to mirror God in our own lives, but to reflect into the world the grace which we receive, and thus mediate the life of God to the rest of creation. When this occurs, it represents a move from simply being a Christian World Viewer to being a Christian World Doer; allowing Christ to work through us, doing small things with great love, solving real-world problems and making a difference in our world for Christ.

For students, it is my hope that you will dare to engage in conversations with your faculty and members of the campus community. I encourage you to think about the journey you are on and the academic community to which you belong. Today, think about what you desire from your studies and experience, live into your educational experience with the end in mind and then make decisions that can lead you there. To me, one of the most foundational decisions you can make is to fully own this time and be willing to engage in the community.

Ephesians 5:15, says "Be very careful then, how you live, not as unwise, but as wise, making the most of every opportunity." Don't simply mark time chronologically while you are in college but seek those moments that are appointed by God and live into this time. When you do, you will discover rich times, times of depth, times that will shape you into His image and lead you into His desired future and life for you.

Choose to wisely invest your time in your educational experience and it will return much more to you than you ever dreamed—intellectually, spiritually, and socially. This part of your journey is unwritten. When you look back, it will be filled with a life shaped by the decisions you make—decisions that will form the story of your life's headline from the days you were in college.

Institutional and individual ownership, and engagement in conversations that matter will not only propel students to achieve a level of professional achievement and personal success but also provide an opportunity for significance and influence, it will enable them to reflect the promise of God and the hope of influencing our world through transformational change that helps to usher in the Kingdom of God.

Dr. Hawthorne, thank you for writing this book to not only inspire us to embrace and embody the very best of what it means to be a Christian university, but for the challenge you offer to fully invest in the experience and discover all that God has for our future—institutionally and individually.

Daniel J. Martin
President, Seattle Pacific University

Preface

This book provides you an introduction to life in a Christian university. I explore a number of questions, share stories, give advice, and connect to some big questions that are part of higher education in today's society.

Here's a bit about who I am (some of which I'll unpack along the way). I am a sociologist by training and outlook. You may not have had a lot of sociology in the past, so I'll try to explain it as we go. For now, just know that I'm fascinated with the patterns of life, how they shape us, and what we can do to control them rather than be controlled by them.

I love thinking and talking about the patterns of life. That's what motivated me to spend my life in education. As a Christian scholar, I care deeply about the Christian faith and how that gets expressed in the next generation. So that's why I've spent my career in Christian universities.

The first half of my career was spent in the classroom, engaging students. The second half of my career was spent in administration, working with faculty to build strong programs that impacted students. Now I'm back in the classroom, which I love. I've now served five different Christian institutions in five states: Olivet Nazarene University (IL), Sterling College (KS), Warner Pacific College (OR), Point Loma Nazarene University (CA), and Spring Arbor University (MI).

I wish I could sit down and hear your story: your hopes and dreams, what got you to where you are today, and where you think you're headed. A key theme of this book is that the Christian university can empower you to pursue the fulfillment of your story. You just need to know how to do it.

Here's what I'd like from you as a reader. Don't agree with me. Write questions in the margins. Engage. As we'll see later, you can take a passive approach to learning and do what's expected to get through a course. Resist this option, even if it's worked well for you in the past.

Instead you can make all you do about your own journey toward the future. That means going beyond what teachers or authors say. It means asking questions, thinking from new perspectives, and taking risks (the good ones).

Unfortunately, we can't know each other personally. But we'll see that the Holy Spirit is leading us to all truth. We'll find that community comes from our common response to Grace. In some way, then, we're connected as author and reader. I'm thankful for your own story and pray that my reflections can help you make the most of its future chapters.

Acknowledgments

I am deeply indebted to many people over the years who have listened to the premise of this book, who encouraged me to keep going, who read drafts, and who shared lots of coffee. Thanks to my colleagues at Warner Pacific (most notably Cole Dawson and Dennis Plies), at Point Loma Nazarene (especially David Whitelaw, Dean Nelson, and Rob Thompson), and host of colleagues at Spring Arbor over the course of the writing (but especially Jack Baker, Matt Hill, Jeff Bilbro, Tom Holsinger-Friesen, and Robbie Bolton).

The family of David McKenna, through their sponsorship of the McKenna Scholar Award at Spring Arbor and through David's commitment to Christian Higher Education, played a significant role in supporting the book. Thanks also to the selection committee and administration at Spring Arbor, especially former president Charles Webb. Thanks to the Communitas Program at Calvin College that hosted me during the writing of the first half of the book in the summer of 2012 and for the many statements of encouragement from summer seminar participants. Thanks to my sociology colleagues at Spring Arbor (Jeremy Norwood, Lloyd Chia, and Lori McVay) for putting up with my distractions as the project unfolded.

I have benefitted immensely from the careful editing the book received. Maggie Tibus was diligent in providing emerging adult eyes to make sure my voicing was right. She was especially helpful in catching my anachronisms when she would kindly say, "I don't know who that is" or "nobody is named that anymore". Thanks to Dick Etulain for his support on an earlier draft. Thanks as well to Christian Amondson and his team at Wipf and Stock for their support for the book and patience as it was coming together.

I am thankful for the support of my wife Jeralynne and for the many hours we've spent talking about Christian Higher Education over the years. I've allowed the book to consume the past two summers and hope we can find time to travel again.

Acknowledgments

Finally, I am indebted to scores of Christian university students over the years that helped frame the basic argument of the book by the questions they asked and their willingness to engage the complexities of life as an expression of their devotion to Christ. They didn't settle for easy answers but wanted to push hard to own their perspectives. Again, there are too many to name but a representative group includes Scott, Christian, Step, David, Jeff, Jana, Jen, Amy, Niki, Cassie, Heather, Matt, Andrew, Bethany, Steve, Mykahla, and Libby.

John W. Hawthorne
Jackson, Michigan
Fall 2013

1

Introduction

Welcome to the start of your adventure into the world of higher education! As Obi-Wan Kenobi told Luke Skywalker, "*You've taken your first step into a much larger world.*" Orientation is over, tearful goodbyes are wiped dry, and you've begun to find a group of folks to hang with. As we will see, this isn't quite like anything you've done before, and yet parts of it seem very familiar.

Transitions can be difficult. We move from what we were sure about to not knowing what it all means. There's a great illustration of a difficult transition in the book of Acts. It is the story of Peter's vision in chapter 11:

> Now the apostles and the brethren who were throughout Judea heard that the Gentiles also had received the word of God. And when Peter came up to Jerusalem, those who were circumcised took issue with him, saying, "You went to uncircumcised men and ate with them." But Peter began speaking and proceeded to explain to them in orderly sequence, saying, "I was in the city of Joppa praying; and in a trance I saw a vision, an object coming down like a great sheet lowered by four corners from the sky; and it came right down to me, and when I had fixed my gaze on it and was observing it I saw the four-footed animals of the earth and the wild beasts and the crawling creatures and the birds of the air. I also heard a voice saying to me, 'Get up, Peter; kill and eat.' But I said, 'By no means, Lord, for nothing unholy or unclean has ever entered my mouth.' But a voice from heaven answered a second time, 'What God has cleansed, no longer consider unholy.' This happened three times, and everything was drawn back up into the sky. And behold, at that moment three men appeared at the house

in which we were staying, having been sent to me from Caesarea. The Spirit told me to go with them without misgivings. These six brethren also went with me and we entered the man's house. And he reported to us how he had seen the angel standing in his house, and saying, 'Send to Joppa and have Simon, who is also called Peter, brought here; and he will speak words to you by which you will be saved, you and all your household.' And as I began to speak, the Holy Spirit fell upon them just as He did upon us at the beginning. And I remembered the word of the Lord, how He used to say, 'John baptized with water, but you will be baptized with the Holy Spirit.' Therefore if God gave to them the same gift as He gave to us also after believing in the Lord Jesus Christ, who was I that I could stand in God's way?" When they heard this, they quieted down and glorified God, saying, "Well then, God has granted to the Gentiles also the repentance that leads to life." (Acts 11: 1–18)

I will leave it to others to explore the greater theological significance of this vision beyond the call to extend the Gospel to the Gentiles, including us. For our purposes in understanding the Christian college, three ideas need elaboration. First, even though Peter was a righteous man, the voice from heaven told him not to call common what God had made clean. The understanding of God was broader than the understanding of Peter.

It is a real temptation for all of us to shape our worldview around our own prior, comfortable understandings of life when God is saying, "*kill and eat.*" We need to remain open to what new insights might be coming.

Second, Peter makes a bold statement in explaining his newfound understanding: "*who was I that I could stand in God's way!*" He arrived at this understanding through a very logical process of being attentive to the connections between what Jesus had said and what Peter experienced. It is an affirmation that God is present in surprising ways and places.

Third, when the other apostles hear the story they praise God and make a bold pronouncement of the larger meaning: "*Then God has granted to the Gentiles also the repentance that leads to life.*" They change their life-long perspective on the basis of Peter's witness. They have been with Peter throughout their ministry and they have seen him struggle to understand Jesus' teachings. Because the apostles know Peter's character, trust his integrity, and carefully consider what he has seen and done with Cornelius, they open themselves to a much broader vision of the Gospel.

Peter's story underscores that we must always be open to change. We recognize that the world is larger than we thought and that our previous answers might need some examination (hopefully in the midst of supportive others).

You've chosen to make your transition into the larger world at a Christian university. Given my background, I obviously think that's a good thing. And yet we will see that things are more complicated than they appear. We'll reflect on the context of your educational journey, the nature of the institution you're joining, how to form community without abandoning identity, how to make the most of your learning, and how to dream about your future. We'll end up seeing that the Christian university is really about practicing the Kingdom of God.

For those of you who attended Christian high schools, there may be some similarity with your last couple of years. For those who came from public high schools, being in a place where everyone is so openly Christian in their assumptions, language, and even Facebook posts may feel comforting and strange at the same time. If you were homeschooled, you are combining a larger number of transitions: leaving home, having teachers you aren't related to, and the temptations of a free and open social life.

The freshman transition requires work. Nobody really has it down. Those who pretend that they know all the ropes (because of siblings at the school or past contacts) truly are pretending. They have questions and uncertainties of their own. Most importantly, we recognize that we're all in this together and will support each other through those changes.

Right from the outset, your experiences prior to coming to college shape in a very real way that we can all make this transition together. In my first class session in Introduction to Sociology, I ask students to get into groups according to the forms of schooling they experienced. I divide the class into those who were homeschooled, those who attended Christian high schools, and those who attended public schools. First, they share within their group what their experience was like. That part of the class is filled with comments like, "Did you participate in co-op debate?" "Did your school have a dress code?" or "How did you like being in a large school?"

After my students spend a little time discussing in their groups, I give them an opportunity to find out what it was like to be in one of the other groups. If you went to a Christian high school, what would you like to ask a homeschool kid? If you were homeschooled, what have you always wondered about what it was like to go to the big public high school?

My sociology class is a small example of a much larger vision of what Christian higher education should be all about. Your experiences are part of the mix. So are my experiences. So are those of every other student, professor, staff member, coach, and administrator in the university. We simply need to make space to explore stories together in the midst of the educational experience.

It is the immanent God working through His Holy Spirit that makes it possible for us to live "*in the world and not of it*" (John 17:13–19). God is at the center of the Christian University, not just as a subject of study but also as the dynamic presence leading to learning.

My classroom example underscores that one of the essential elements of our life together is telling our story. We aren't just like everybody else. We are unique creations, with experiences and perspectives that help shape who we are. It is, then, in the actual sharing of life that our community is built. It's also the way the educational practice should work.

Our common work doesn't end with your story. It only begins there. When your story interacts with that of your roommate, of the person sitting next to you in speech class, of the professor teaching history, or of the characters in the book you read in literature class, we can start to build some larger understandings. That cooperative and collaborative effort should be at the very center of our work.

Daniel Taylor, in his wonderful book *The Healing Power of Stories* (Taylor, 1996) argues that every story involves a writer and a reader who each bring their unique individuality into interaction. He observes that when we read a good story, we don't just identify with a character but rather we move alongside the character. To the extent that our situation is similar to the character in the book, our understanding is deepened and our life situation can be changed, even by a fictional relationship. We join into the plot, at least vicariously, with similar impacts. Particular movies (or characters) shape how we all see the world as well as your own individual sense of self.

Consider the Harry Potter series of novels as an example. A generation of young people have read these books and used them as mirrors of their own relationships and personal development. That this series moves a compelling set of characters through the complicated transitions from children to adolescents creates a backdrop to which all children can relate (especially since they aged at the same rate as the characters).

If we react to stories in this fashion because we understand plot and character development, Taylor says we also relate to our own experiences as story. The story into which we are born has been in development for a long time when we join the plot so we join the flow of action that is already underway.

Stories help you imagine situations that aren't immediately available to you, evaluate what you'd do if you were in such a situation, and compare your views with those of other readers. The recent fascination with *The Hunger Games* trilogy seemed to take over college campuses in ways that helped people explore ideas of obligation, inequality, fashion, and violence.

Your presence in your story also changes the flow of the plot as it unfolds. Your younger sister is born into a very different situation than what you were born into because there's another person to interact with. When you leave home to go to college, the family story starts a new chapter and the plot is different if you live at home than it is if you live on campus.

Here's some of my college story. My educational journey began in a state school, Purdue University. When it was time for me to pick a college to attend, I looked only at the school ninety minutes from my house. My grandfather had graduated from there and I had admired the school (particularly the football team and the marching band) throughout my youth. It just seemed natural that I would head north upon my graduation from high school.

Perhaps a Christian college could have been an option. To be fair, even though I was a Christian and involved in school-based activities like Youth for Christ, I didn't have a church home.

I found myself as a freshman studying mathematics in a state school. All in all, my professors never did anything to challenge my upbringing or faith positions. My dorm-mates enjoyed socializing like any other college students but Purdue has never been known as a "party school." I knew people who were heavy partiers but they weren't difficult to avoid.

If I had fit into Purdue's system and moved properly through my educational experience, life would have progressed well. I simply would have moved through the institutional system as most students do (we'll explore the limits of this strategy in the next chapter). So I attended classes (most of them) and turned in my work (nearly always). I struggled to manage the freedom that college brings: going to class or sleeping in, doing homework or playing cards. Looking back, I was probably lost shortly after I arrived. By the end of my first semester, I was on academic probation. Thinking that maybe the problem was my major, I switched. At the end of my second semester, I was academically dismissed. The dinner conversation with my family about how this high school honors student could flunk out of school is one of those burned into my memory.

The story of my first year of college helps frame a key approach taken in this book. Understanding my story helps you understand the narrative arc that provides meaning, motivation, and direction to the ways I interact with the world. So it is with your story and everyone else you run into at college.

One of my favorite stories is the plot for Frank Capra's *It's a Wonderful Life*. You get several opportunities to see it every Christmas, but its meaning is more profound than just as a heartwarming Christmas Eve story. The hero is George Bailey, the oldest son of a family in the little town of Bedford Falls. George always wants to leave Bedford Falls but puts his own wishes behind what is needed by others, thereby changing the lives of those around him. He keeps the town banker, Mr. Potter, from destroying the family building and loan that is the only place for the "little man" to have access to owning a home. Eventually the building and loan runs into a financial crisis (not George's fault but he takes responsibility). With all other options exhausted and at a particular point of deep frustration he considers jumping off a bridge to commit suicide. He is visited by an angel and given the gift of seeing how the world would be if he had not been born. He finds that his impact on relationships changed the character of the entire town and all of its inhabitants. Through this experience, he discovers, in the words of his guardian angel, that "*one man touches many lives.*"

A parallel story could be told about the banker, Mr. Potter (although it would not make such an inspiring Christmas tradition). His greed, his need for control, and his thirst for power harmed all the people who interacted with him or his institution. Corruption, selfishness, and greed all followed in his wake. What would the town have been if Mr. Potter had not been born? It is likely that people whose lives had been crushed by his abuse and power might find their lives instead opened to new dreams and possibilities. Maybe another George Bailey would have revolutionized the community.

Such a little change contains the potential to revolutionize everything. The closing scene of the movie *Back to the Future* provides a beautiful illustration of this point. George McFly (Marty's dad) finally stood up for himself at the prom in high school against the bully Biff. As a result, his home is now nicer, he's a published author, his children are successful, and he's a better parent.

Colleges have stories as well. Certain events can become the master narrative against which all other experiences are evaluated. Some schools that are defined by a history of financial struggle may not know how to respond to success when it comes. Other schools wind up viewing all events through the prism of a particularly tumultuous political period in the distant past. Sometimes the narrative is offered as a contrast with what happened to some other institution. We will see that the secularization of the once-religious Harvard University is often offered up as a negative example of what can potentially happen to Christian colleges.

Contrasts between religious and secular views of the world are not new. In some ways, it's the story of the church in society. Sometimes, however, events help clarify the assumptions underlying our perspectives.

We can get a glimpse of these tensions by looking at the Scopes Trial in Dayton, TN in 1925 (see (Larson, 1997)). Three-time presidential candidate William Jennings Bryan traveled to Dayton, Tennessee, to argue in favor of the state law that outlawed the teaching of evolution. Using a rigid biblical interpretation, he argued that the evolutionary approach would undermine individual faith and moral order. Nationally known defense attorney Clarence Darrow defended John Scopes, the young biology teacher who had agreed to challenge the recently passed Tennessee law outlawing the teaching of evolution.[1] Darrow served as the example of progressive, rational learning. His defense depended upon the use of our "modern" approach to scientific empiricism (what philosophers call "positivism"). Journalist H. L. Mencken, who had established himself as a critic of religion in the press, covered the trial with relish. His picture contrasted the calm, scientific view of Darrow with the fundamentalist mindset of Bryan. Although Darrow provides a major critique of Bryan's point, the facts of the case (Scopes never denied teaching evolution to his high school students) and their own backgrounds caused the jury to convict Scopes. Even though Darrow lost the case, his position was established as the socially dominant worldview.[2]

When the Christian college attempts to take matters of faith seriously as an educational topic, it is met with a key question from its secular counterparts: *How can one be a good scholar and seriously consider such topics?*

1. An interesting side note to the story is that the ACLU took out ads in the paper looking for communities to challenge the law. Dayton accepted and encouraged Scopes to go ahead and teach evolution to force the case.

2. The play and subsequent movie, *Inherit the Wind*, is based upon this event. While it obviously loses some detail and exaggerates the differences between the two positions, it does a good job of illustrating both the intellectual tensions between the lawyers and the cynicism of the journalist.

As we will see in chapter four, this question even occurs to Christian college faculty as part of our graduate school training. Furthermore, when the Christian scholar approaches topics that are standard fare within secular institutions (the evolution question in the Scopes trial is a good example), it is done with a similar degree of suspicion: *How can one be a good Christian and seriously consider such topics?*

This book[3] seeks to establish a unique role for Christian higher education in this postmodern world.[4] As we will see, what is happening in your world is very different than what was happening when I was in school. We need a means of thinking about Christian higher education that is brave, open, and engaging.

In modern culture, we are continually forced to divide the world into a black and white mode. Much of life is squeezed into a set of yes or no boxes. If you turn to cable news or talk radio, you will find hosts who love the president and those who despise the president, regardless of which party is in power. Economic life pits owners against workers. Religious life separates mainline Christians from fundamentalist Christians. In the abortion debate, we're given the option of being "*pro-life*" or "*pro-choice*". Education often seems like a battle between teachers and students or between teachers and administrators.

Some commentators would readily suggest that such an argument is what's wrong with our world. Academics, they say, are especially to blame and just should learn to see Truth in the world and not make everything so complicated. The preferred strategy seems to be to hold to one's position regardless of its logical conclusions or difficulties in implementation. It's as if there are more points awarded for being consistent (but incomplete) than

3. There are other scholars of Christian higher education who have written on worldview approaches. Good examples can be found in *Conceiving the Christian College* (Litfin, 2004), *Shaping a Christian Worldview* (Dockery & Thornbury, 2002), or *Faith and Learning on the Edge* (Claerbaut, 2004). Others prefer to think of "ecclesial colleges" that follow the form and function of monastic life. Two good examples of this approach can be found in *Desiring the Kingdom* (J. K. A. Smith, 2009) and *Conflicting Allegiances* (Budde & Wright, 2004).

4. Postmodernity is a complicated concept meaning different things to different scholars. In short, postmodernism assumes the enlightenment view of the world (which we call modern) is supplanted by a viewpoint that puts priority on individual values. It moves away from an assumed commonality of values.

dealing with the world as it is (in its messiness). Past generations might have been willing to oversimplify the world to make it fit existing views. Not so for your generation that came of age after 9/11. You've learned that the world is messy and are asking how that affects your education.

I am suggesting that we need to see an infinite variety of solutions from which we work out a particular path. From a mathematical perspective, it may be that there are a number of logical possibilities along a continuum but some are better than others. In physics, certain vectors allow for better flight than others. Imagine an air traffic controller working through a series of minor adjustments when advising a pilot about the best way around a thunderstorm. As Christians, we have faith that we are being led by God's spirit and not flailing about on our own.

A principal feature of the doctrine of the Trinity is that the Holy Spirit actively influences our understandings in the period since Christ ascended into Heaven. Whether issues involve questions of the continuity of the church over the generations, the changing political structures in the Reformation or Vatican II, or emerging connections between faith and science, there is a positive role played by the Holy Spirit. This is an important corrective to both a purely enlightenment view (entirely dependent upon rational decisions) as well as a conservative view (unwilling to consider new ideas that might challenge previous understandings). The presence of the Spirit allows the Christian university to operate from a stance of fearlessness precisely because we are committed to obedience to the leading of the Spirit.

Let's return to Peter's story from the beginning of the chapter. How he and the other disciples responded to God's leading provides a fascinating model for adjusting how we think about faith and learning. It suggests the important role that complexity plays in our understanding. Peter is holding to his deep belief that he should be faithful to God and he is also completely open to what God is teaching him. It is not possible for him to choose only one of these options. He must be simultaneously embracing both.

In fact, even using Peter's story illustrates my point. As a sociologist and educator writing about the philosophy of Christian higher education, how can I use scriptural example as a model? I'm far more likely to argue, "*Lord, you know I am an academic and have always built careful and theoretical arguments based on the best scholarship.*" But maybe the Lord says back to me, "*Don't ignore what I have given you; read and consider.*"

Let me suggest a different parallel with the story of Peter's vision. Consider one of your friends beginning school with you as a first-time freshman attending this Christian university. All his life, he has studied the Bible and tried to understand its application to his life. He has heard good preaching and taken it seriously. Perhaps he attended a Christian high school and was well versed in apologetics. What will be in his sheet let down from heaven? Perhaps it comes when he is asked to read about the origins of the gospels in a Bible class or must read an existentialist writer in English class or take seriously the theoretical perspective of Karl Marx in a sociology class. His response will be like that of Peter: "*Surely not, Lord! Nothing impure or unclean has even entered my mind.*"

Such a student will struggle through the initial shock, just as Peter struggled. We should make sure that he doesn't have to do so alone. Peter says he had six believers with him when he went to see Cornelius. It is necessary to have trusted colleagues (students and faculty members) available as one is working through new understandings. The student is also challenged to find the consistency between this new understanding and what he has learned of God in the past. And when he explains that new understanding to his friends, to his faculty members, and especially to his parents or pastor, they must carefully hear, evaluate, and respond as the other apostles did for Peter.

Peter's story is central to the educational task of the Christian university. From the time you first hear about a college, you need to know that you will likely confront many ideas different from what you've experienced in the past. All aspects of the college life should be focused on providing a trusting environment within which you open yourself up to new learning.

You must have a sense of trust in those faculty and staff members who create the supportive environment. The work of confronting these new ideas is as disorienting for an eighteen-year-old as Peter's vision was for him.

To maintain your trust, you should expect the faculty and staff to maintain three consistent orientations. First, in their own Christian exploration they must articulate how they are continually learning. Not only are they willing to move outside their normal comfort zones but they are willing and eager to engage others in how they react to that movement.

Second, those who form the institution must be continually affirming their Christian commitment in the face of the new learning. They must be able to model for you the ways in which their faith is vibrant and fearless and is never something that needs to be guarded. The idea that the Christian faith must be protected from various writings, opinions, theories, or perspectives suggests that God could not hold us firm. Such a position is the exact opposite of what Peter experienced. Instead, he and the other disciples affirmed that their faith was dynamic; new ideas could be incorporated to what was already believed in ways that strengthened the resulting faith.

Third, the faculty and staff must look to you to learn what it's like to be eighteen or nineteen years old. This is the apex of the process of individuation, where you are learning who you are as opposed to who you've been told you are. This time of exploration and experimentation must be handled with extreme care.

For those of us who are well beyond eighteen, it can be hard work to remember what it is like to try to live on one's own and to be free to create one's own successes and failures. I share my college failure story with students in part to let them know that failure is not terminal. But in a much more important way, sharing my story is to remind myself who I was at eighteen so that I can empathize with their struggles and questions. This is a significant point because eighteen-year-olds face the temptation of transferring parental authority to whatever professionals they attach to in the college setting. It is not the task of faculty and staff to tell students how to solve their quest for meaning but simply to support them while they pursue the appropriate quest one pursues at eighteen.

The heart of the educational enterprise in a Christian university is your unfolding story pursued simultaneously with the unfolding stories of all your classmates. The critical elements of institutional success are not based solely on high graduation rates and strong GRE scores, although these are important byproducts. The most important challenge of the Christian university must be to provide a place in which you can live out your story in ways that are sensitive to God's leading, academically grounded, faith affirming, and celebratory of your unique identity.

2

What Am I Doing Here?

It may seem awfully late to ask this question. You've already selected a Christian university, said goodbye to the folks, begun to get acquainted with your roommate, and started attending classes.

And yet, are you simply getting caught up in the flow of these events? You picked a Christian school because your parents thought it was a good idea, the state school was just too big, your friends at church were going, your grandparents didn't want you around "bad behaviors." Sometimes it's easier just to move on to the next stage in life without a lot of reflection on choices.

It shouldn't surprise you that there are many different yet valid reasons why you're here. Those different reasons may pull in different directions sometimes, reflect the views of some segments of your world and not others, and generally put you in a place where it seems hard to please anyone. It's worth unpacking these different perspectives so that we can see how they operate.[1] If you can see all the roads before you, you can make better choices along the way. (Hopefully, our reliance on GPS and Google Maps hasn't made that metaphor outdated!) Putting all the options in context and figuring out how to proceed is actually a key lesson of liberal arts education at its best.

---

1. I first came across the idea of examining rationales for education in Neil Postman's *The End of Education* (Postman, 1995). He refers to his rationales as "gods" but I'm borrowing the technique throughout this chapter.

The State of Higher Education

There has been an assumption for most of my career that higher education was a good thing. Partly because of the GI Bill providing educational benefits to veterans coming back from war and helping to fuel the growth of the middle class, we have seen larger and larger percentages of graduating classes consider some form of higher education. An expanding economy seemed to thrive on newly minted college graduates.

Sure, there were problems. Critics cited professors who delighted in promoting extreme views in their classes and feared that indoctrination was more significant than learning. Other reports cited surveys of employers complaining about the poor writing skills of college graduates. Still others critiqued the tenure system as a way of propping up lazy professors who were well past their prime. The media, especially the twenty-four-hour cable news channels, delighted in these stories even though they were true in only a very small percentage of cases. No one reported that most tenured professors worked hard, that many students did extraordinary work, or that most professors tried to avoid indoctrination and preferred careful reflection. While these critiques were rarely directed at Christian liberal arts institutions, all of higher education got thrown in the same pigeonhole.

Something changed in the early 2000s. First, the budget shortfalls in many states caused them to drastically reduce the money they'd set aside for higher education so public universities and community colleges had to drastically raise their tuitions, lay off faculty and staff, and reduce class offerings. Second, federal budget challenges limited the growth of Pell grants. When combined with the tuition increases, it pushed a larger share of the student financial burden from grants to loans. Third, the rapid growth of for-profit institutions drew upon those limited federal financial aid funds and elevated the role of "quick and convenient" education. Fourth, the struggling economy made the job market for new graduates more uncertain. Fifth, certain high profile issues around college professors (e.g., Colorado's Ward Churchill) dominated some sectors of the news media and became symbols for what was wrong with higher education in general.

Any one of these shifts would present a challenge to higher education. Taking them together in such a short period was devastating. When the Occupy Wall Street movement began in the fall of 2011, there were far too many placards that read "*$125,000 in college debt, unemployed.*" There has been much quality research on the factors that contribute to higher tuition rates, changing faculty work situations, student aid limitations, and the like. It's enough for now to simply suggest that there are no easy causes and fewer easy solutions.

This became clear during a recent presidential campaign. The president, advocating for the importance of a college education as a lever toward jobs and upward mobility, had suggested that everyone should pursue at least a year of college or trade school. One person, seeking the nomination of the opposing party, had suggested that the president wanted everyone to have a college degree and commented: "*What a snob!*" I'm not advocating for a party here, but the disdain with which college education was viewed (by someone with advanced degrees, no less) was certainly a shift.

There is something behind the federal or state policy shifts regarding higher education. These abrupt changes occurring within about a decade is really about our confusion over the purposes of a college degree. While Christian colleges are not uniquely affected by all of what I've described, we suffer from the broader confusion.

Let's turn our attention to exploring four of those visions of higher education and see why they matter. My guess is that you'll find your own answer to the "Why College?" question in some combination of the following ideas.

Answer #1—It's the Next Step on the Journey

This answer is so basic that when folks ask you when you decided to go to college, you're actually kind of stumped. You've always known you were going to attend; maybe even this particular school! It's as if you were carried along with the current. Sure, you could have changed course if you wanted but the path seemed to work for you so you came along.

One thing sociology teaches me is that even when I know what's going on, I align myself to the expectations of others around me and adjust to the institutional dynamics I find myself in. This is the story of my first year at Purdue. It ended badly because I hadn't stopped to consider what I was doing. I was just fitting in and going with the flow of the current.

All my students have heard me talk about the Three Big Transitions. I sneak it into nearly every class. The First Transition occurs when you start school. It may have been pre-school, Sunday school, or kindergarten (it works differently if you're homeschooled.) The second transition occurs when you leave your home, friends, and church and move to the college campus. The third transition is your transition to independence after college.

Before you started your schooling, it had been you and your parents (and maybe a babysitter). You did what you wanted, within reason. Your time was your own, for the most part. The basic rule was to keep your parents happy with you most of the time and enjoy your development. Then we sent you to school. Suddenly, your time was structured for you. You didn't get to decide what to do or when. And this person up in front of the room got to tell you what to do. She (usually a she) didn't know your parents, didn't live at your house, and probably didn't go to your church. But she still got to decide what to do and when to do it. If she said it was naptime, it was naptime. If you were told to sit on the rug for reading time, you'd better sit on that rug.

It's bad enough for you to have to deal with strange authority figures. But your performance was under scrutiny. How well were you meeting the expectations of the teacher (and those others you didn't even know who defined those expectations)? It's also critical to know how well you're measuring up to the other students in the class. Are you falling behind? Jumping ahead? Compared to the others, do you need extra help? Are you suspected to be "gifted and talented"?

Every once in a while your parents are asked to come to a meeting where your teacher can report on your progress. After all these years, I still remember the meeting where my first grade teacher wanted to hold me back because my handwriting was bad (still is). My parents insisted that I be allowed to move on. Then we moved; maybe they didn't win the argument after all!

Do you recognize the picture I'm painting? School becomes a massive institutional effort organized to evaluate your performance, sort you by skill, and move you forward to the next set of tasks. Maybe this is why reality shows like Survivor are popular. They remind us of the hoops we jumped through throughout our schooling.

The picture gets more complicated the further along you are in school. The complexities of the middle grades are very different from those early years. I've always believed that we specially groom stern fourth grade teachers to wean you from the notion that you have to like the authority figure! Along the way, you are tested and tested to make sure that you are gaining ground (because we want to hold schools and teachers accountable). Junior high school adds the newfound power of peer groups and hormones and you begin learning that you have to deal with competing demands all the time. High school pushes you to new levels, but once you sort yourself out into groups (even without Harry Potter's sorting hat!) you figure out what's expected. And if you move forward through all this institutional life and stay (mostly) out of trouble, you'll find yourself wearing a robe and shaking hands with the principal.

Then your mind turns toward college. You hopefully gave a lot of thought to where to apply. Ideally, the school you're attending was at or near the top of your prospective list. You applied, got accepted, and attended the pre-registration session that introduced you to college and let you pick your classes (or at least approve what was picked for you).

It's hard to overstate the power of the Second Big Transition. Most of you had to physically move from the home you have lived in for awhile, maybe for your whole life. You've left behind friends and routines (you'll write about them on Facebook but it won't be the same.) You'll have a roommate you may have chatted with over the summer and you'll find new friendship groups. You'll make your way to classes, keeping your schedule handy for the first couple of weeks. (If you were home schooled, you get to do both transitions at once!)

In the classes, your professor will hand you a syllabus and tell you what must be done and when. You'll quickly look at the major paper or exam dates and hopefully write them down in your scheduler/phone/iPad. You might look at the grading scale and gauge how this class will be compared to the others you're taking.

You'll try to balance the demands of the first class with those of the second and so on, asking questions like, *why do all the exams happen at the same time? Don't they know I'm taking other classes?*[2]

Even with that uncertainty, you'll fall into a routine. You can do that because the shift to the academic part of the Second Transition is the easiest step. The work may be more demanding but it's still teachers telling you what to do when and measuring your performance against a set of standards. You won't get as many reminders as you did in high school and you will find extra credit exceedingly rare. If you're struggling in class, it's incumbent on you to go for help. Folks aren't going to seek you out as much.

The big challenges you'll face have to do with how you manage your freedom and independence, how you balance academic life and social life,

---

2. Because if we all give three exams and there are fifteen weeks in the semester, we all divide the same way and get five. Yes: deal with it.

and what Christian faith has to do with any of this. We'll come back to this in Answer #3.

Because you have spent twelve years immersed in the educational system, you know the ropes. You figure out what's expected and manage to do your best. Well, at least you manage to do enough of your best. Doing your best might require more effort than you've put in before.

You'll try getting by until you don't get by. This is why the national data on student studying is so awful. According to a recent book on the problems in higher education by Richard Keeling and Richard Hersh (Keeling & Hersh, 2011), *"studies show that on average undergraduate students are doing a mere 10 to 15 hours per week of homework while receiving grades of B or higher in their courses"* (p. 36).

Here's my big confession—we created this situation, you didn't. We in higher education have focused on making it clear exactly what's required of you. We do it in classes, we do it in majors, and we do it in the university as a whole.

I know the drill as well as anyone. In my institution, it takes 124 hours to graduate. You have to have forty upper division hours. You must have a 2.5 GPA in your major and a 2.0 overall. You must have an appropriate configuration of general education courses. You have to watch out for prerequisites and get your grad check done by the required dates.

We have focused on the wrong things. We've built systems for tracking your progress toward completion and other systems to intervene if you have difficulty. We create checklists for you to cross off courses (in my institution we have a computer program that checks it off for you.) By focusing our energies on the mechanisms of navigating college life, we've distracted you from college life. We've made education about a convenient system.

A focus on systems too often pushes us to look at the wrong things. We ask questions about the percentage of students who come back after the freshmen year or the percentage who graduate within six years (for private institutions nationally, those figures run roughly 67 percent and 64 percent, respectively). These are important questions for administrators to ask and are truly important for how the university views itself, but they rarely lead to initiatives that can impact the decisions of a particular student. Similarly, universities worry about the impact of grade inflation. Stuart Rojstaczer and Christopher Healy analyzed grade data from 1940 to 2008 (Rojstaczer & Healy, 2012). It's a complicated statistical analysis, but the following results stand out: 1) there has been a significant increase in the percentage of A grades over the last forty years, 2) this seems fairly related to the students who are recruited (higher ACTs are related to higher grades), and 3) there has been an abandonment of the previous focus on a standard curve centered around the C+ grade. Most colleges and universities reflect what's called a "bimodal distribution," with a group of students in a cluster at the top range of grades and another a little lower (in the C to B- range).

Clearly, such data merits some attention and careful conversation about overall statistical patterns. But, this is too often part of the institutional thinking that takes us further down the road toward credentials as the desired end point without attending to means of getting there. I'll come back to this when we get to Answer #4, but for now it's worth mentioning that a focus on individual learning asks a different set of questions.

Our focus on "getting people through the system" feeds an overall consumer mentality pervading our culture, including higher education. We want happy "customers" who have their needs met.

The past two decades have seen tremendous growth in for-profit schools like the University of Phoenix. They have been successful by marketing to a population of students who want to get their degree but have trouble balancing their family and job. So they have short classes at night, on weekends, or online. My institution does this as well.

But when our focus is on checking boxes on the big audit sheet, on navigating the insides of the institution of higher education, we weaken the entire learning project. We create situations where it's reasonable for you to ask if you can get by on two hours per night studying. We set up conditions where you can passively put in your time.

At the end of the day you'll still get your credit unless you really mess up. If you do "enough" to get the minimum acceptable grade, you get to move on. In my most cynical moments, I think we're playing Who Wants to be a Millionaire? You made it through Intro to Sociology! Want to stop now or take a chance on English Literature?

Obviously I'm not satisfied with this answer, but I have to acknowledge that it's where some of you are starting. At this point, I return to the previous section and ask, "*If you're investing a hundred grand, shouldn't you get something more than the participation trophy?*"

Answer #2—I Need a Job

One of the motivations for going to college is highly utilitarian: a means to an end. We need a higher education because it's essential to "Getting a Good Job." You major in a given field because it's the best expression of your interests, skills, and passions. At least that's why you should major in it.

Some students begin the college years with a commitment to a particular type of employment. Maybe it carries high prestige or demands a high salary. Perhaps it reflects the hopes and dreams your parents have had for you. I remember a student who wanted to be pre-med because that's what would make his father happy, but the student soon learned that he didn't like lab sciences. I've known people who thought about education because they liked the idea of summers off, but they weren't creative and didn't particularly like children.

The problem with a means-to-an-end approach to your college years is that it puts all your focus on what's coming later. You get so committed to that imagined end that you can't truly enjoy what you're doing at the moment. In addition, any disruption in plans (like that B- grade in Intro to Sociology) is a direct threat to the imagined end-point.

Wait a minute, you might say, the cost of four years of education at a Christian university will easily exceed $100,000![3] I can't lay out that kind of money only to live with my parents and deliver pizzas. If that's the goal, I could have done that right out of high school.

Of course you can't. The higher unemployment rates for young adults in our challenging economic times underscore how hard it can be to find that first job. Two factors can add more context to our discussion.

First, our economy experienced some significant shifts in recent decades. The jobs available to many workers at the end of World War II didn't require college degrees. *The Atlantic* produced the chart on the next page illustrating how employment patterns shifted from 1947 to 2009 (Thompson, 2012). It contrasts the percentage of total employment made up by each sector (in other words, the figures should total to approximately 100 percent on both sides.)

The chart shows what we probably already knew, but it does so dramatically and visually. Look at the changes in some of the sectors. You'll see that three sectors (manufacturing, wholesale/retail, and agriculture) saw

3. This is a rough estimate. I took the average cost of a year at a private school (around $30,000) and then backed out the amount granted in scholarship aid, which is really a discount to the "sticker price" and multiplied by four.

their share of the jobs shrink by a combined 26 percent over the sixty-two years. Where did those jobs go? Another three sectors (finance, professional, and education/health/social services) saw their share of jobs increase by a combined 26 percent. There is little doubt that the areas of potential employment that didn't require higher education have shrunk for a variety of reasons (it has a lot to do with technology and increased productivity.) Those areas that have grown in popularity largely require education beyond the high school level, especially if advancement is to be possible.

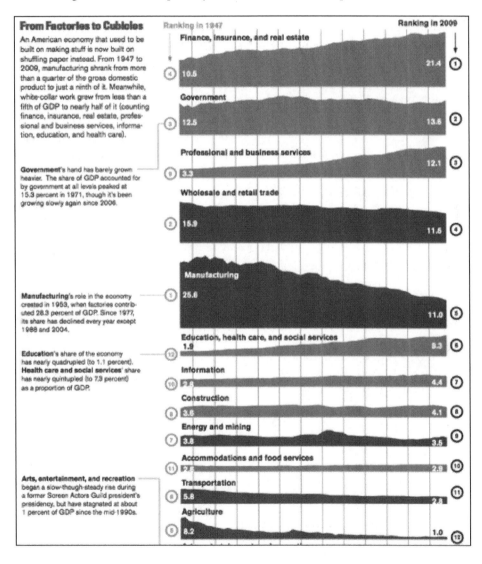

The other factor connecting higher education to jobs is the curious tendency for employers to equate a college degree with the ability to use technology. One of the byproducts of having so many companies, even Starbucks and Target, using computer technology is that employers exaggerate the skill level necessary to work there. If one has to manage computerized inventories, they argue, then some familiarity with statistics and decision-making are needed. Of course, this is partly a reflection of the technology gap between the generation that hires and your generation. You've literally grown up with technology and are not afraid to simply dive in and make sense of it. Did anyone read the instructions to the newest video game before starting play?

Nevertheless, the data connecting earning potential to college education is nearly indisputable. In 2011, Tiffany Julian and Robert Kiminski conducted a Census Department analysis based on data collected from 2006 to 2008 (Julian & Kiminski, 2011). Through some complicated statistical projections, they estimated "synthetic" lifetime earnings for various levels of educational achievement. It's synthetic because they didn't actually measure what someone earned but looked at what statistical expectations would be within a reasonable margin of error. Their report breaks down the data by race/ethnicity and gender.[4]

I've summarized their data for the White, non-Hispanic population in the graph below. It shows the significant impact over one's lifetime of work. The results are nothing short of striking.

Julian and Kiminski estimate that the average high school graduate will earn $1,690,285 for males and $1,183,917 for females. The numbers change dramatically once one completes college. For students with bachelor's degrees, the estimates jump to $2,847,953 for men and $2,028,096 for women. The potential gain over the course of one's lifetime stands at $1,157,668 for men and $844,179 for women.[5] In terms of lifetime earnings, a college degree is worth an additional 67 percent for men and 71 percent for women.

4. Unfortunately, they didn't include a summary statistic regardless of ethnicity and gender. The data for different ethnic and gender groups reflect the general patterns but lag behind for reasons too lengthy to explore here.

5. The gain for Hispanics is $773,811 for men and $680,545 for women. For African Americans, the comparisons are $767,321 for men and $788,552 for women.

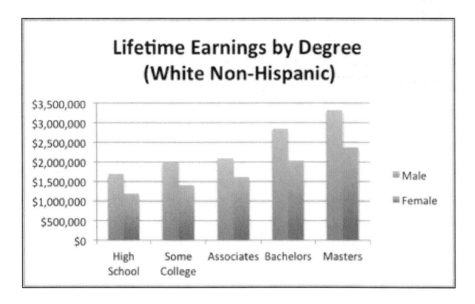

Lifetime Earnings by Degree (White Non-Hispanic)

Remember that we estimated the costs of a four-year degree to be roughly $100,000. That means that the value of pursuing the college degree and the jobs it might lead to pays for itself between eight and eleven times. While it doesn't make paying for college any easier, it does help to take the long view.

Two more things before we leave this topic behind. First, I need to point out that the job focus is only part of the story. Each year the Higher Education Research Institute (HERI) at UCLA conducts a study of incoming freshmen across the country. The number one reason for nearly 86 percent of those going to college in 2011 was *"to get a good job"* (Pryor, DeAngelo, Blake, Hurtado, & Tran, 2011). But *"to learn more about things that interest me"* was number two at over 82 percent. These aren't directly competing goals but they still need to be harmonized (more on that later).

The second thing you need to keep in mind is that this whole section deals with two different things: a good job and lifetime goals. Those are not the same thing. Our obsession with jobs, especially in a difficult economy, has led us to a short-term time horizon. It's not your first job you're getting ready for, but the one seven to ten years down the road. You aren't just looking for a job to pay your school bills but a career that fulfills a calling. The real question is, *"where can you invest yourself to make a difference?"*

This is the difference between job, occupation, and vocation. You should strive to find an answer to this larger vocation question: *what are you called to do?* One of my favorite books is *Wishful Thinking* by Frederick Buechner (Buechner, 1993). Buechner summarizes the vocation search like this: "*The place God calls you to is the place where your deep gladness and the world's deep hunger meet*" (p. 119). Keep your focus on that and the job and money will follow.

Answer #3—The Security of a Christian Environment

There are positive and negative reasons to choose a Christian university, although many students might collapse all of these into a phrase like "*Christian community.*" Even though there is far more diversity in a Christian university than you might expect (we'll deal with this at length), many students come to college assuming some measure of similarity with others. Depending upon your particular denominational background, if any, you may have known some fellow students from summer camps or other collective activities. Perhaps you even agreed on a roommate at one of these events, so that you weren't a total stranger when you got to campus. Even though we will see that you are far less likely to get married in college than previous generations (so we can end the lousy "*getting your MRS degree*" jokes), there is value in exploring potential relationships with those who share a great deal in common with you (religion, geography, social class). You look forward to worshipping together in chapel with friends, sharing your faith journeys, and ministering side by side. All of these dynamics can make a Christian university very appealing.

Almost all Christian universities are residential in nature. In short, you get to share life. Ernest Boyer, the former U.S. Commissioner on Higher Education who attended Messiah College and Greenville College, conducted a major study of American higher education in the late 1980s (Boyer & Carnegie Foundation for the Advancement of Teaching, 1987). It remains influential to this day, as does most of his work. He highlights that the social aspects of university life are significant simply if one looks at the clock:

> There are 168 hours in a week. If a student takes 16 credit hours, and spends 2 hours in study for each credit hour of instruction (a generous estimate!), that means that 48 hours of the week are devoted to academics. If 50 hours are assigned to sleep, that leaves 70

hours[6] in the student's life unaccounted for, a block of time greater than either sleep or academics. (180)

It is natural, then, that being in community is highly valued for faith-based institutions. Boyer reported that four in five students interviewed from religious institutions felt a strong sense of community. Another educational expert, Alexander Astin, of UCLA (part of the group that does the freshmen survey we saw earlier), echoes the values of a residential community (Astin, 2000):

> In many ways, the philosophy underlying the notion of a liberal education in a small college setting is a tribute to the power of the peer group. This form of education implicitly assumes that an excellent liberal education is much more than a collection of course credits, and that a little bit of serendipity is a good thing. Allow young people to go away from home and live together in an intimate academic environment for a while, and some good things will happen. Often we really have no idea what these good things will be, but the students will seldom disappoint us. (p. 98)

It's important not to overstate the similarity that you might find in that peer group. It may be that you feel like you aren't quite like the others. Maybe you went to a different church, or rarely went to church at all. Maybe you have a different set of interests. Maybe your sport is very demanding and takes up a lot of your seventy hours of free time, or perhaps you don't "get" music people but love artists. Maybe you were forced to attend this school, at least for a while.

Political scientist Robert Putnam wrote *Bowling Alone* to examine how modern Americans connected to each other (Putnam, 2000). He reminds us that we need to be focused on the building of two different forms of social capital: the resources we use in cooperation with others. One form he calls "*bonding capital.*" This results from the similarities and interactions that connect us to one another. We enjoy each other's company and so we do things together. Then we tell stories of "*that great time when we did that thing,*" which deepens the bond. But Putnam says we also need the "*bridging capital*" that connects us to other groups and makes us feel part of the larger whole. You find the bridges when you learn that you know some of

---

6. The free time in college is certainly a temptation that robs other pieces of the college experience. So I was stunned recently to see a television commercial from Dell offering a free Xbox 360 for any computer purchased for college. Do these even belong together?

the same people or you sat near each other in that one math class. To make the most of the residential community you've chosen, both forms of capital are really important.

Those are the positive reasons: similar folks, a sense of connection, common values. What were the negatives? These are harder to get at because you don't actually experience them. Instead, they form part of what shaped your overall decision. It's what is called a *"counterfactual."* How would your life be different if you'd gone to that large state university where some of your friends went? What might that have been like? Surely, the Christian university must be preferable to that secular environment!

It's not hard to paint the picture of life in the big state school. Some images of it are well grounded in reality. Others simply reflect isolated stories that have been passed down. There are numerous Christian books out there (you may have gotten some for a graduation present) encouraging you to keep your faith in the midst of a hostile environment. You are warned about *"secular humanist"* professors who will regularly attack and belittle your faith. You'll hear stories about those Christian young people who went off to college and lost the fire of their faith.

I don't want to minimize this issue. There are some isolated professors out there who would engage in such behavior. Not to put too fine a point on it, but they are jerks who simply like to hear themselves talk. It's not good teaching to attempt to demolish the faith of a student any more than it would be appropriate for me to single out a non-believing student in class as a point of ridicule. But most professors will focus on their material and raise appropriate questions you might not have considered. Actually, that's going to happen in the Christian university as well.

As I've already told you, I'm a product of one of those big secular universities. The sociology professors knew me, knew my testimony, and treated me like a human being. I was never once held up for scorn even in a discipline tempted by relativism or economic determinism.

There are great Christian students at secular schools. Campus ministry organizations like InterVarsity, Campus Crusade, the Newman Center, and a host of other denominational groups provide a safe place for Bible study and Christian fellowship. There are good Christian professors at state schools.[7]

---

7. A group I belong to, the Association of Christians Teaching Sociology, changed their name twenty years ago from the Society of Teachers in Christian Colleges to welcome those Christian faculty in state schools.

The hostile professor is just one of the negative images of the state school. The others have to do with the very strength of the peer group that Alexander Astin was celebrating. A significant part of campus life in major institutions involves decisions about sex, alcohol, and frequently both.

Some recent research by sociologists has uncovered some of the challenges of these behavioral choices. In an expansion of her dissertation, Kathleen Bogle contrasted sexual expectations at a major state school and a smaller Catholic institution (Bogle, 2008). Not only did she find that sexual attitudes are far more fluid among today's students, but she suggests that a large campus helps the hook up culture. There are a lot of people to run into and the odds that you'll see each other again are slim (much less so at most Christian universities). She spends a lot of time discussing the ambiguity of what "hooking up" even means and how women are still at a significant disadvantage. She also makes clear that many students aren't involved at all, even at large schools. She concludes by expressing some concern about the relationship between sex, alcohol, and power.

Two other sociologists took a look at how students make sense of the culture of alcohol on campus. If you've ever seen the movie *Animal House*, you are aware of the image of the drunken college student (if you haven't, there are many other images of student parties in the media). As it happens, both of these sociologists begin their books with a description of John Belushi's character in the film. In *College Drinking*, George Dowdall examines the relationship between alcohol abuse and other problems like academic struggle, date rape, and crime (Dowdall, 2009). He goes on to encourage students to examine college policies toward alcohol and available campus support services as part of the college selection process. The work of Thomas Vander Ven moves the analysis from the social problems to how students define their choices regarding alcohol (Vander Ven, 2011). His conclusion is instructive in light of the peer group pressure we discussed above:

> The college experience fosters beautiful friendships that can last a lifetime, and the world of adventure that alcohol facilitates is often the primary context of those friendships. Maybe drinking episodes are not the ideal concerns for relationship building and character development. *Maybe we have done our children a disservice, somehow, by making them so self-conscious that they think they need alcohol to interact freely and confidently with others.* (p. 182, emphasis mine)

Even with this data, we need to recognize that there is a significant percentage of students at the big state school who don't drink. Some of these have made choices for healthy living and others are focused on potential legal action that could affect future employment.

Two more things about the behaviors at the state school. First, the behaviors we've been reviewing happen at Christian institutions. Not as much, certainly, but they are still there. You can find folks who drink. You can look for hook up opportunities. In fact, Kathleen Bogle found that there were only minor variations of the hooking up theme at the smaller Catholic liberal arts school she studied when compared to the large state school.

I once worked with a campus pastor who started the school year telling the students, *"If you're looking for it you can find it here."* In all cases, you need to know what to do about that. How will you address them? How can you build connections with others that protect you from the excesses of your new-found freedoms?

Here's the second thing. The patterns of behavior described by these sociologists didn't just begin the first day of school. Early in my career, I conducted a nation-wide study of Christian college students in which we found that not only had a significant number been active sexually and involved with alcohol, but they had been doing so for at least a year before college. Their pastors and parents may have been unaware (at least they pretended not to notice!), but the peer pressure that's in the friendship groups is certainly active throughout high school.

In other words, secular institutions aren't all dens of inequity in spite of news stories about extreme cases. Christian institutions aren't all places of purity, in spite of what our admissions material might say. The peer group with whom you bond and those other folks with whom you form bridges can influence your behavior for good or for ill. Trust me. Those peer relationships are why I flunked out of school.

It's an important part of life in a Christian residential university, but it's not all there is. All three of the reasons we've examined so far help frame the final reason you've come to school. Each of them is foundational to the big task you're really involved in: the task of becoming who you were meant to be. That's the focus of the final and most important reason for coming to college.

Answer #4—Preparing for my place in the world

That may not be the way you would have phrased it. Early in my teaching career, I wouldn't have phrased it that way either. I would have said the point was to "learn stuff." I would teach the sociology class because I love it and my goal was to get you to love it too. Somehow, I was always disappointed. When someone's hand shot up in class for a question, I'd prepare myself for an interesting discussion about the implications of the lecture point. Invariably, the question was more in the spirit of, "*Can you repeat the second point?*" On my more depressing days, the question was, "*Does this have a point?*" (Actually, that only happened once but I've lived in fear of it ever since.) And, of course, there was the inevitable, "*Do we have to know this for the test?*"

My views on the purpose of education shifted over the past fifteen years. One of the motivations was reading Neil Postman's book mentioned in the footnote above (Postman, 1995). Postman got me thinking about what we were trying to do in Christian higher education. One line has always stuck with me, particularly during my days as an administrator:

> What are schools for? . . . What is all the sound and fury about? If a metaphor may be permitted, *we can make the trains run on time, but if they do not go where we want them to go, why bother?* (61, emphasis mine)

Shortly after reading Postman, my colleague, Lou, addressed a group of incoming freshmen the summer before starting school. He picked out one student (we'll call him Larry) and said that Larry may be thinking that he's taking four classes: Composition, Sociology, Bible, and Art. In fact, Lou suggested, Larry is taking four classes in Larry! He wanted Larry to understand that his entire college experience should be considered forty-one classes in Larry.

Right around the same time, I was observing a class a young professor was teaching. It was tough material and he was a compassionate teacher. But he was moving at a very rapid pace. I asked him, "*If at the end of the semester, you're the only one still getting what's going on, what would we have accomplished since you knew it already?*" That was a turning point in one of my fundamental understandings of education: It's not about me.

It's not. I really do want to introduce you to the wonders of sociology (they're right there for anyone to see!) But at the end of the day, my classes have to mean something to you personally. If not, we've just gone through the boring motions of racking up three more credits. But if your view of the world gains a little clarity, if you understand your roommate or your parents just a little better, if you're able to talk calmly about major political choices—in short, if you are a better person than you were before the course started—then we've been part of something remarkable.

Such ambitious goals for our time together in class run directly counter to the assumptions we saw in the first three reasons for coming to college. Working toward that first job, completing required credits, or biding your time until you can hang out with your friends simply doesn't lead to the kind of personal growth and development I'm talking about.

In fact, our inability to make that transition may be behind some of the most significant critiques made of higher education in recent years. Derek Bok was twice president of Harvard University and is a significant scholar of higher education. In spite of the glowing reputation of major research universities, Bok provided a remarkably thoughtful critique of undergraduate education (Bok, 2006):

> Even among the selective colleges that are ranked so highly and attract so many applicants, *fewer than half of the recent graduates believe that college contributed a "great deal" to their competence* in analytic and writing skills or in acquiring knowledge of their major fields of study. . . . Surveys of student progress in other important dimensions, including writing, numeracy [math], and foreign language proficiency, indicate that only a minority of undergraduates improve substantially while some actually regress. (p. 311, emphasis mine)

Bok goes on to explain that we really don't know enough about what makes for good teaching and good learning. Most professors, even those at Christian universities, received little training in actual classroom teaching. The training we received in our disciplines dwarfed the little instruction in pedagogy we might have received. It's why we get tempted to treat our students like they should aspire to be college professors! Bok remains sympathetic:

> The great majority of professors enjoy their teaching, like their students, and devote much time to their classroom responsibilities. Yet enjoying teaching and caring about students do not necessarily bring a willingness to reexamine familiar practices and search for new methods that could serve the purpose better. Indeed, the opposite is often true, at least for professors whose classes are going reasonably well. (p. 313)

In short, your professors are doing their best to communicate the material based on their training. There is a surprising amount of trial and error in college teaching. I'm frequently frustrated in the knowledge that things are not going how I want them to and I wind up tinkering with pacing, discussion, content, anything (!), to find something to break me out of my rut.

Can you see how a faculty member's approach to teaching intersects with the bureaucratic approach to racking up credits toward a degree? Even if we're going along, doing our best without really developing meaningful learning, the system still works: grades are recorded, credits are earned, prerequisites are met, and degrees are granted. But we've missed a remarkable opportunity.

This is why I've made this critique of higher education such an important part of this chapter. It's hard to change a culture. For reasons we've already seen, it's far easier to go along with what's been before. "If it ain't broke, don't fix it," the adage goes. But it may be that we're simply pretending it isn't broke because that's easier than fixing it. You see, if we focused on your learning and created the contexts where that is central to what we do together, it could change the entire dynamic of the Christian university.

In one of my favorite books, *To Know as We Are Known* (Palmer, 1993), Parker Palmer critiques an objective view of knowledge designed to hold things at a distance (what Keeling and Hersh would call pedestrian) and to see the importance of learning that interacts with your search for meaning.

> By Christian understanding, truth is neither "out there" nor "in here," but both. *Truth is between us, in relationship*, to be found in the dialogue of knowers and knowns who are *understood as independent but accountable selves.* This dialogue saves personal truth from subjectivism, for genuine dialogue is possible only as I acknowledge an integrity in the other that cannot be reduced to my perceptions and needs. (p. 55–56, emphasis mine)

Palmer is saying some fascinating things about your learning. Not only does he see it as dependent upon your processing the material through your own experience with an open mind, he sees that the learning of your classmates is dependent upon that as well. Even more significantly, it's essential to my effectiveness as a college professor. It's in the authentic interaction around our learning together that higher learning occurs. Harvard English professor Louis Menand (Menand, 2010) puts it this way:

> Historical and theoretical knowledge, which is the kind of education that liberal education disseminates, is knowledge that exposes the contingency of present arrangements. It unearths the a prioris [those things taken for granted] buried in present assumptions; it shows students the man behind the curtain; it provides a glimpse of what is outside the box. It encourages students to think for themselves. (p. 56)

I love what Menand is suggesting. By inviting you into the educational process as a participant, it becomes a part of your life. It's part of your story, the raw material from which your future options unfold. This is what my colleague meant by "forty-one classes in Larry."

Let me tie this together as we end this chapter. We've looked at four reasons for selecting a college: getting a job, pursuing the credential, finding a community, and developing higher learning. In reality, I want you to think of them the other way around. The first question is about how the university allows you to grow. Your classroom experiences become the raw material from which you are broadening and developing. In doing that, you are helping your fellow students and your professors to do their own broadening and developing. As you take responsibility for one another, your social capital strengthens with those around you. You have a vital reason for making choices (and avoiding bad ones like hooking up and binge drinking). Your choices impact those around you, hopefully for the better. Along the way, you'll be taking classes that have become meaningful and in the process, not worry about grades and credits. And because you've lived in community with others and worked to navigate difficult waters, you'll be standing head and shoulders above all those other people who are applying for those jobs and building their careers. You won't have to be trained to solve problems because you'll already be a creative problem solver.

By understanding your personal responsibility for your own growth within the college setting as the primary task of college, you come to rely on the leading of the Holy Spirit to help you work through differences with others, grasp new perspectives, and critically engage the world.

3

Your Generation Is Different

About the time school starts each fall, Wisconsin's Beloit College releases a "mind-set" list for the incoming freshman class (Troop, 2011). It's a reference to factors in popular culture, technology, and politics that shape the experience of the incoming class. Most students entering college in the fall of 2011 were born in 1993. This means that students like you see things differently than previous classes—and certainly different from your professors! A sampling of the Beloit list suggests that most freshmen in 2011:

1. never saw Michael Jordan play basketball,

2. never saw the communist party in control in Russia,

3. didn't use dial-up internet,

4. have always had access to charter schools,

5. have only seen major labor disputes in major league sports, and

6. don't know that Brittany Spears and Justin Timberlake started out on the Mickey Mouse club.

The list stands in stark contrast to my own experience. Jordan changed professional basketball. The USSR was a dominant threat throughout my upbringing. There were major labor disputes pitting government against workers. Getting any kind of computer access through any means was a major breakthrough for a young professor. Disney Channel wasn't around until my children came along (and then it was a premium channel).

This is not simply to suggest that I'm getting old, although that's certainly true. In fact, if I assume that your parents were between twenty-five and thirty when you were born, then your parents could have been in my first classes when I started teaching. At least I'm not finding grandchildren in my classes!

Generational changes are clearly more important than keeping up with pop singers and athletes or new technologies. They truly reflect some major differences in the world we inhabit. Because the best learning takes place in the context of one's prior experience, the changes occurring in the culture are worth attending to. Your generation has been exposed to a much more complicated world than earlier generations. That makes cut-and-dried answers harder to handle.

Sociologists, journalists, and other commentators find it useful to define labels for different generations. We use titles like Baby Boomers (born between 1945 and 1964), the Greatest Generation (born in the Depression and becoming adults during World War II), or Generation X (born in the early 1980s). These labels certainly don't describe all individuals in the age group, but such cohorts[1] do let us examine the impact of certain changes in society during the time one is coming of age.

The Baby Boomers have received tremendous attention in recent decades. The sheer size of the birth group relative to earlier groups has created major ripples across the nation. We built schools then consolidated them as the boom passed. We created suburban developments of box-like houses that then deteriorated over time and were replaced by newer, bigger, more up-scale developments for their children. Their retirement and health care issues are major challenges to containing Medicare and social security costs. Because they are a large voting block and have significantly longer life spans than earlier generations, they've probably deserved such focus.

Our focus on the Boomers may have led us to believe that their patterns would continue in future generations. But sociologists have noticed some interesting societal shifts coming along in the wake of the Baby Boom generation. Your generation is waiting longer to marry (if they do), is more geographically mobile, more likely to attend college, and generally in less of a hurry to achieve the major markers of adulthood. Robert Wuthnow (Wuthnow, 2007) cites data from a MacArthur Foundation report on young adults:

1. Sociologists use the term "cohort" to refer to all people born in a particular time frame. We can think of it as similar to generational labels popular in the media but it has a slightly more technical meaning.

> Comparing statistics in 2000 with statistics in 1960, the research-
> ers found, for instance, that completing all the major transitions
> (leaving home, finishing school, becoming financially indepen-
> dent, getting married, and having a child) was achieved by only
> 46 percent of women and 31 percent of men age thirty in 2000,
> compared with 77 percent of women and 65 percent of men of the
> same age in 1960. (p. 11)

A number of factors contribute to this sense of delay. Longer life spans change one's time horizons: Wuthnow observes that fifty now marks the true middle of the adult's life experience, being halfway between twenty and eighty. A shifting economy has limited options for younger workers while increasing the demand for college degrees. Increasing opportunities for women outside the home change the balance between career and family. As corporate and organizational structures have moved from local to national, geographic mobility is always on the horizon. Changing sexual attitudes have disconnected sexuality from marriage for many in society.

In late 2011, the Pew Research Center (Cohn, 2011) analyzed 2010 U.S. Census data showing that the median age for marriage had increased to just under twenty-nine for men and just over twenty-six for women. As shown in the graph on the next page, the median marriage age is now approximately one year later than just ten years prior.

What are the implications of the six-year lag in median marriage age over the past fifty years? How do these societal shifts create a context for students like you? As we will see, these shifts are far more significant than sports stars, celebrities, or even political alignments.

Emerging Adulthood

Psychologist Jeffrey Jensen Arnett has been exploring these questions since the beginning of the twenty-first century. He advocates the need to define a new stage of developmental psychology that he calls "emerging adulthood" (Arnett, 2004). While the beginning stages of emerging adulthood correspond with high school graduation and the possible move to college or university, the upper limit is harder to define.

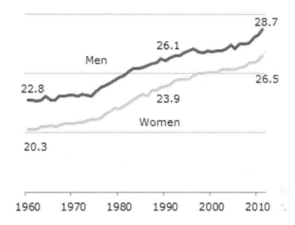

Median Age at First Marriage, 1960-2011

in years

28.7

26.1

Men

26.5

22.8

23.9

Women

20.3

1960   1970   1980   1990   2000   2010

Source: Current Population Survey, March and Annual Social and Economic Supplements.

PEW RESEARCH CENTER

Arnett asked students what would tell them that they had achieved "adult" status, having them select from a list of options. In the vast majority of cases, the accomplishment of adulthood was related to issues of independence from parents, responsibility for one's actions, and developing personal positions on matters of values. In contrast, no more than 40 percent of students chose issues related to "rites of passage" (drinking age, marriage, graduation, birth of a child, first job).

This period of life that you are now in, which Arnett says cannot be considered as simply continuing adolescence, is characterized by five components. Based on his research, he finds that emerging adulthood is a period of identity exploration, an age of instability, a self-focused stage, a period of feeling "in-between," and a time of possibilities.

When you moved onto the Christian university campus the week before classes began you didn't use Arnett's descriptors or think of yourself as "emerging," but you may clearly embody the components he describes. The start of school is the point at which you can re-invent yourself: a new hairstyle, the Christian tattoo on your foot, a new nickname, and/or the selection of a different kind of crowd to run with. The sense of instability is almost instantaneous as there is so much to learn that others seem to know.

Or you may find that over this first year you switch majors a couple of times, change friendship groups monthly, join a worship band and then quit, and try out several dating relationships to see if any have sticking power. You are comfortable with experimentation because there is little permanence to what you are considering. That becomes less true over time —at some point continued experimentation and uncertainty gets in the ways of progress toward academic, spiritual, or relational goals.

What Arnett is suggesting is that the apparent fluidity that frustrates parents and professors alike is actually a characteristic of the developmental stage you find yourself in. In spite of all the varied good things the university is trying to do (academic development, spiritual grounding, social relationships, vocational clarification, personal growth), it is still happening in the context of the larger psychological dynamic. As we saw in the last chapter, this life stage corresponds to the Second Big Transition, one of the most radical social transformations you will ever face: leaving your home of origin and discovering independence.

Students like you have been shaped by the broader context of life for eighteen-year-olds in the early part of this century. Different students will certainly experience these larger contextual issues to a greater or lesser extent depending on their family circumstances. It matters if you were urban or rural, whether you went to public school, Christian school, or were homeschooled, and whether your parents were college educated.

In today's rapid media environment, there is less insulation than in prior decades. It's worth exploring some of those broader trends and then returning to the implications for you as a Christian university student.

To set a larger context, we need to look at some recent research on religion in America, especially as it impacts the under-thirty population in general. We will see that there are some distinctive things happening among "the younger generation," with a dramatic rise in the percentage of those claiming no religious connections whatsoever. Next, I want to explore some data out of the National Survey of Youth and Religion that explore how eighteen to twenty-three year olds think about their faith, how it gets tied up in a variety of conflicting values, and what that might suggest for Christian universities. Finally, a review of recent research by the Barna Group on the struggles that Christians in the eighteen to twenty-nine age range face within the institutional church will show how much the struggles of the emerging adult intersect with religious life. In general, these three pieces of research tell us a great deal about what's going on in the lives of the emerging adult population, how they think about religion (when they do), and what that might suggest for you as a student in the Christian university.

Shocks and Aftershocks

In 2010, Robert Putnam and David Campbell authored a massive and massively important book on religion in America (Putnam & Campbell, 2010). Although the book has an intriguing title, *American Grace*, the subtitle may be even more important for our current discussion: How Religion Divides and Unites Us. Putnam and Campbell combine interviews, visits to local churches, and careful analysis of survey data from the General Social Survey (a very reliable survey of American attitudes that has been repeated over decades).

Putnam and Campbell argue that the decade of the 1960s was pivotal in American Religion. The multiple streams of major social currents disrupted an apparently calm and complacent post-war 1950s. Using the metaphor of an earthquake to describe these shifts, they then examine two "aftershocks."

The first was the rise in evangelical dominance (especially numerically) during the 1970s and 1980s.[2] The aftershock, as the authors see it, was an attempt to restore balance after the disruptions of the previous decade. When coupled with the decline of the mainline Protestant churches (largely due to age), evangelicals seemed an important force. They provided significant push back on the perceived liberal stances of the 1960s (especially, the authors argue, with regard to premarital sex). The rise of evangelicals led many to argue that people wanted more conservative direction. Early in this period, a church leader named Dean Kelley wrote a book making this claim (Kelley, 1972) and the next decade of research in the sociology of religion was devoted to exploring Kelley's thesis.

The second aftershock described by Putnam and Campbell occurred over the past twenty years. While the evangelical period was characterized by conservative theological and moral values, there were many, especially among the young, who saw this is an overreach. Survey data began showing increasing concern over strident voices among the religious community, especially the popular leaders. While the data does not significantly

2. This was a period of tremendous growth for Christian colleges and universities.

distinguish between evangelicals and others, this shift takes place following the rise of major evangelical media figures like Jerry Falwell and James
Dobson.[3] There really weren't many major religious figures arguing for
moderation in the 1990s.

While they don't connect their data directly to the emerging adults,
it's not surprising that the concerns about traditional sexuality might create
a backlash among those trying to figure out who they will be as adults and
how to make decisions for themselves. Regardless, Putnam and Campbell
view the second aftershock as being even more significant than the first.

By looking at changing attitudes and behavior by cohort (contrasting
those who were a certain age in one decade with those of the similar age
in another decade), the shifts present in the second aftershock take on a
dramatic form. Consider the following graphs from the book:

ESTRANGEMENT FROM RELIGION AMONG COLLEGE FRESHMEN (1965–2009)

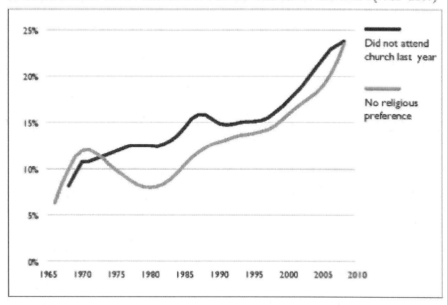

SOURCE: THE AMERICAN FRESHMAN ANNUAL SURVEYS; DATA LOESS-SMOOTHED.

This graph shows the percentage of college freshmen in different time
periods that had no religious involvement at all. While it's important to

3. Falwell was the president of the Moral Majority and Liberty University. Dobson
was the founder and long-term president of Focus on the Family. Fallwell died in 2007.
Dobson ended his affiliation with Focus in 2009.

recognize that the percentages on the left axis only run up to 25 percent, it's still a remarkable shift in nonbelief since the end of the first aftershock (which is the little bump in the attendance line). The percentages move from 15 percent to 24 percent in the space of just twenty years.

EVANGELICALS AND "NONES" AMONG AMERICAN YOUTH (18–29), 1973–2008

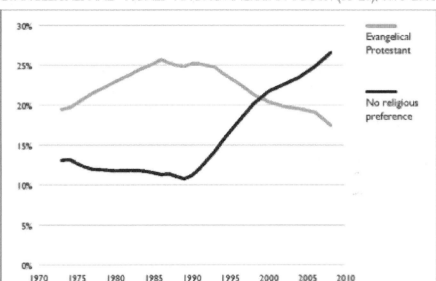

SOURCE: GENERAL SOCIAL SURVEY; DATA LOESS-SMOOTHED.

This graph includes our emerging adult population, regardless of whether they are in college or not. Between 1995 and 2010, the relative proportions who reported being evangelical or "none" reversed. Where the evangelical young adult population outnumbered their nonreligious counterparts by roughly 7 percent (23 percent to 16 percent) at the beginning of that shift, by 2010 the nonreligious were up by about 10 percent (27 percent to 17 percent).

Putnam and Campbell don't argue that evangelicals pushed people out by being strident. But it is clear that a change is going on that impacts both of the groups in the second graph. As it has become more socially acceptable to claim no religion at all (thanks in part to the rash of "new-atheist" books on the market), evangelicals may rightly feel embattled. A brief review of any webpage's comments concerning articles on the role of religion in society will show as many people defending religious orthodoxy as attacking it as the source of all of society's ills.

These changing social trends are not a surprise to you, even if they might be to your parents, pastors, and professors. You've seen this throughout your schooling. You have had these conversations in your classes, been challenged by what you had to read, engaged in intense discussions in high school with teachers or peers, or had a feeling that the local pastor is just a little too certain while the students are in an age of exploration.

What do you do in these situations? If you are like most students, you react by avoiding discussion. You may be afraid to give "the wrong answer." You may not know how to engage the dialogue in a productive way without simply adopting the view of whomever you heard last. But you are unlikely to challenge the assumptions of those around you.

It's essential that you do so. It is imperative that all aspects of the Christian university—its culture, its faculty and staff, its curriculum, its extracurricular activities—recognize the tenuous place you are in your journey and make it possible for you to explore all possibilities. To do anything less fails to take education seriously.

National Survey of Youth and Religion

Another strand of research sheds more light on what might be happening in the religious lives of young adults in a postmodern society. Beginning in 2003, a team of researchers led by Notre Dame sociologist Christian Smith began exploring the religious lives of American teenagers in a project called the National Survey of Youth and Religion, or NSYR. The first survey was conducted when the teenagers in question were between the ages of thirteen and seventeen. The results of this study are summarized in *Soul Searching* (Smith & Denton, 2005). The NSYR is special because it's a longitudinal study; most of the young people involved in 2003 were interviewed again five years later, when they were eighteen to twenty-three. This age range roughly corresponds with the college-aged portion of the emerging adult population. Sociologists and religious educators sifted through the results of the second wave of the survey to see how religion was affecting the lives of modern young people. While most subjects were not Christian college students, their attempts to make sense of religion and morality help define the context of this generation of Christian college students.

The second NSYR book, *Souls in Transition* (C. Smith, 2009), offers insights and identifies some specific challenges facing the eighteen to twenty-three year old population. It comes as little surprise that the major themes Smith and his colleagues discovered in their in-depth conversations align with the general themes that Arnett describes. The young adults in the NSYR were focused on the transitions of their lives, about the state of their relationships, the implications of their past decisions combined with an interest in moving on, sorting out the moral ambiguities of a complex society, and separating from parents without abandoning them.

One of the striking things the interviewers discovered was the strong view of individualism the subjects expressed. While this is consistent with Arnett's "self-focused" age, relying on the individual's own viewpoint (as opposed to traditional or institutional sources) is intriguing. This same sentiment is given to others in a sort of reciprocal understanding; I can only decide for me and you can only decide for you. Smith describes this sentiment:

> The words *duty, responsibility,* and *obligation* feel somehow coercive or puritanical. Saying that somebody "should" do something is about as far as many emerging adults are comfortable going. You can't make anybody do anything, so don't even try to influence them. Stick to what you think is right. Tell others what you think, if they ask you. But respect the fact that everything is finally the others' own call. (p. 49, italics in original)

Such a "live and let live" sentiment is dominant but not universal in emerging adult culture. It is true that some students come to college with very firm views on things and challenge anyone who doesn't support their views. But because the very nature of the emerging adult period is one where peer acceptance and fitting in are especially important, many students are in a much more flexible situation. When this power of the peer group combines with the relative distance from parents or home church, we can see the resulting sense of self is more fluid.

How does this relate to views on religion? The interviews suggest that many emerging adults don't think a lot about religion, don't talk much about it with their friends, and that religion may be valuable for some as nothing more than a moral guide. In the first wave of interviews, the researchers discovered that many teenagers held a belief that Smith and his colleagues labeled Moral Therapeutic Deism, or MTD. MTD, they argue, has five components: 1) God created an ordered world, 2) people should be nice and fair, 3) happiness is the primary motivation in life, 4) God can be distant unless it's an emergency, and 5) good people will go to heaven. Others in the NSYR research group (Dean, 2010) place responsibility for MTD on parents and churches who failed to develop deeper images of Faith, Church, Salvation, and Kingdom in their own lives and practices. Smith suggests that the life challenges faced by many of today's eighteen to twenty-three year olds might threaten an earlier easy, happy faith in Moral Therapeutic Deism.

A recent book by Smith and his colleagues, *Lost in Transition*, analyzed the same interviews by examining the moral challenges faced by emerging adults (Smith, Christoffersen, Davidson, & Herzog, 2011). They discovered that students had a fear of being judgmental, instead substituting what the authors call "moral individualism." They write: "we discovered that the vast majority of emerging adults could not engage in a discussion about real moral dilemmas . . . (p. 60)." Some of this they lay at the feet of public education, claiming that the "moral pedagogy of most middle and high schools clearly seem to be: *avoid, ignore, and pretend the issues will go away* (p. 62, italics in original)."

It's fair to add churches and families to this list. This cannot be the "moral pedagogy" (that is, the philosophy of teaching) of the Christian university. The moral issues you've been pondering, discussing with your friends late at night, and writing about in your journal must find their way into the classroom where they can be intelligently explored in a compassionate way.

As part of the NSYR, the interview teams spoke specifically about religious beliefs and practices. In analyzing the results, they classified students into six major approaches to religion. First were the Committed Traditionalists; those active in Evangelical, Black Protestant, or Mormon groups for whom faith was very important. The second group they labeled Selective Adherents; those who had some religious background but took more of a smorgasbord approach allowing one to pick and choose beliefs and practices. Spiritually Open emerging adults may have religious background but are exploring many forms of religion. The final three groups have great similarity to what we saw in the Putnam and Campbell data. The Religiously Indifferent don't concern themselves with religion one way or another. The Religiously Disconnected have no prior background with religion. The final category is the Irreligious; these differ from the other non-religious groups in their antipathy to religion and religious folks. Smith and his colleagues attach some rough percentages to the six categories, which I summarize in the pie chart below.

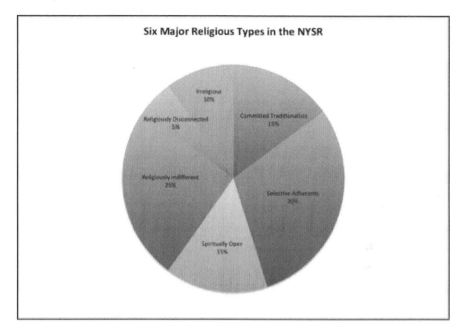

As I said, these are rough percentages so the fact that the three less-religious categories make up 40 percent of the total probably doesn't mean that much. It may be that some part of the Religiously Indifferent group could switch either direction, which would lead to a breakdown closer to the 27 percent non-religious shown by Putnam and Campbell.

In any case, the less religious categories are not likely to be interested in attending a Christian university, even if close to home or a chance to star on an athletic team or drama group. But given our review of the emerging adult literature, we need to recognize the diversity present among the other three groups. Many students at a Christian university may be likely to come from the Committed Traditionalists, but some will be Selective Adherents, and a few others will be Spiritually Open. Listen to your peers describe their reactions to chapel services or a required class in New Testament and you will hear all of these strains expressed.

All of these emerging adults will be shaped to some degree by the larger trends we've been examining within the age cohort. The Committed Traditionalists may find themselves more willing to listen to the views of the Spiritually Open because of the norms governing the way we manage differences. To say the same thing another way, there are significant pressures in emerging adult culture to not come off as judgmental.

This describes one of the primary tensions you experience as a new student: how to handle disagreements. When someone "comes on too strong" in a class discussion, this will often be met with (at least) nonverbal disapproval from others. In my experience, some kind of apology the next class period is not unusual.

The other dynamic that bleeds in from the larger emerging adulthood culture is the sense that a student is only responsible for his own view. In other words, "this is what I believe" can be used as the end of a conversation instead of the beginning point for deeper learning.[4]

Concerns about the Church

In January of 2012 Jeff Bethke, a well-meaning student at Pacific University in Portland, recorded a YouTube video of his spoken word poem, "*Why I hate religion but love Jesus*" (Bethke, 2012). Here's a selection: "*Religion may preach grace but it's another thing they practice/Tend to ridicule God's people, they did it to John the Baptist/They can't fix problems, and so they just mask it/not realizing religion's like spraying perfume on a casket.*"

Unfortunately for Jeff, his amateur video went viral in less than twenty-four hours. As of this writing, it has been viewed 24.5 million times! While I saw many articles and blogs critiquing Jeff for under-developed theology and offering improved ways of engaging his questions, I saw many more re-posts on Facebook with affirming comments and encouragements for others to watch immediately. While I didn't keep careful track, my sociological radar tells me that I could divide the responses to Bethke's poem by the age of my friends. Those who were current students or recent graduates were in favor. Those who were older (especially those with theological training) were disturbed by Jeff's naiveté.

Based on the content of his poem, if Jeff were part of the NSYR interviews he'd likely be somewhere near the border between Selectively Religious and Spiritually Open. The judgmental spirit he perceives from many quarters makes him distance himself from religion (although he ignores a number of places that would express the view he's advocating). Here's the point: it doesn't matter to Jeff that there are those who would disagree with

---

4. We'll explore these issues in later chapters. Community building is the core of chapter 6. Chapter 7 deals with personal development. Chapter 8 is all about learning.

his position. *It's more important that he say it.* It's part of the open experimentation of the emerging adult period. And if he's wrong? It's a learning experience he'll use in future growth.

The Barna group has been studying religious trends within the evangelical community since 1984. Their work originates more in the world of ministry organizations than in the kinds of social science research we've been exploring. But their interests provide a parallel argument to what we are seeing with emerging adults, even those choosing to study at Christian colleges and universities. Two recent books summarize this research.

Barna president David Kinnaman wrote *UnChristian* about the emerging adults who would be on the left side of the NSYR pie chart (Kinnaman & Lyons, 2007). Using his own data sets, he estimated that 40 percent of the emerging adult population could be characterized as "outsiders to Christianity." In their various surveys and interviews, they come across six themes that seemed to define the perceptions of those who were not interested in affiliating with Christians. While individual views of Christianity might not match these broad categories, they are still worthy of examination. Kinnaman and Lyons define these as "very real ways in which the Christian community has presented itself to a skeptical generation." The outsiders see the Christian church as 1) hypocritical, 2) too focused on getting converts, 3) anti-homosexual, 4) sheltered, 5) too political, and 6) judgmental (2007: p. 30–31). The sentiment could be summarized: "if that's what being Christian is about, I don't want it."

These concerns are reminiscent of a story that Philip Yancey relates in *What's So Amazing About Grace?* (Yancey, 1997). He opens the book recounting a conversation a friend of his had with a young, drug addicted mother in desperate trouble. The friend asked the young woman if she'd ever thought of going to church for help. Her reply was chilling: "*Why would I ever go to church? I already feel bad enough about myself. They'd just make me feel worse*" (p. 11).

Four years after *UnChristian*, Kinnaman turned his attention to the students on the right side of the pie chart in *You Lost Me* (Kinnaman & Hawkins, 2011). The authors explore the question of why emerging adults who grew up in the church find themselves moving away from congregational life (but not necessarily faith in Christ) during their twenties. They see the answer, at least in part, in the changing dynamics of youth culture. This is not simply the repetition of a rebellious pattern that every generation faces. They claim that "*our [youth] culture is discontinuously different*" (p. 38) due to technology and other pressures facing emerging adults.

Interestingly, they describe the currents of culture in almost exactly the same ways that Arnett described the struggles of emerging adulthood: 1) fluidity, 2) diversity, 3) complexity, and 4) uncertainty. In other words, the confluence of major cultural trends in society and the psychological dynamics of the emerging adult may be mutually reinforcing, at least for some. They go on to raise concerns about access to modern culture, alienation from others, and skepticism about authority (both personal and institutional). In short, these disaffected Christians find it difficult to remain connected to the churches of their past in the face of modern tensions.

Again, they conduct extensive interviews and come up with six broad themes[5] that help explain why the disaffected are leaving, even temporarily. They identify six problems in the contemporary Christian church in America: 1) overprotective, 2) shallow, 3) anti-science, 4) repressive, 5) exclusive, and 6) doubtless (p. 92–93). They suggest that if the church were to find ways of engaging the emerging adults in meaningful ways, through mentoring, vocation, and service, the young people would find ways through their cultural balancing act. This is reminiscent of Jeff Bethke's poem. He saw these six themes present in churches he knew (or imagined) but not characteristic of Jesus' ministry.

All of this psychological, sociological, and ministry research informs a great deal of what's going on in the lives of a college student during the first weeks of school. As new arrivals in a strange environment, you are overwhelmed with the freedom that lies before you. No parents telling you what to do, no church leaders looking over your shoulder, no high school cliques defining your reality. Sure, Christian universities have lifestyle agreements and resident directors, but it's not the same. This is a time for focusing on who you are and who you want to be. The options are limitless, which is scary.

But you also want to fit in. You fear being the oddball who is too pagan, too religious, too academic, or too political. In many ways you share the concerns of your generation. You may have the same concerns about the church, other Christians, chapel, even your professors. Do they doubt? Are they real? Are they judgmental?

What the NSYR surveys tell us is that there is much to discuss. Too much of American Christianity consists in "safe" conversations with topics and emotions that are okay to talk about. I know this will upset my readers,

5. These themes exhibit some remarkable overlaps with the issues Arnett and Smith see as present with emerging adults.

but I'm convinced that this is why so many of our praise choruses are so internally focused. I recognize that worshipping God is the purpose, but they seem driven to raise the awareness of YOU worshipping God. It's self-focused, internal, and therefore safer.

The mission of the Christian university is to explore the range of challenges. We intentionally want to consider bigger questions during college because we know that you'll face them later. We must be brave and help you run deep roots to your ideas. Chapel and bible study foster growth but it also happens through reading thoughtfully, avoiding predictable answers, and really listening to each other.

One of the things that I've learned about Christian university students over the past ten years is that you're brave; way braver than my generation was at the same age. You've been paying attention to the world around you. You've explored honest conversations with your friends, even if you didn't do so at church or in school. You want to know how to address the economy, gay rights, family stability, global poverty, militarism, justice, and the church.

The worst thing that Christian universities can do is to create little cocoons where you are cut off from the big issues of the day. To do that is to repeat the issues that the Barna group is raising and to leave future generations of Christians isolated from those they want to reach and to run the risk of alienating the very thoughtful Christians who daily wrestle with faithful Christian living. It would mean that we failed in our commitments to prepare you for your futures, where these conversations *will* be a regular part of life.

I often tell my classes, "The difference between your generation and mine is that you don't understand that what you are trying to do is impossible." I mean that. At least according to my generation's definition of impossible. We make lists of obstacles to overcome. You are more likely to act.

You really believe that your time in a Christian college or university is a time when you'll sort out the world's problems and help the church be what she's supposed to be. My job is to support you as you work through all those questions and find the path.

I need to help you find your informed and authentic voice that can speak to your generation in the years to come. In turn, you need to push yourself to ask the hard questions, be willing to make necessary challenges, and to help us be a better Christian university.

A First Step into a Much Larger World

The challenge is that large but we can do it because of the strength you brought with you when you arrived on campus. And because we know the Spirit is leading us to all Truth (John 16:13).

4

"Where I Come From, We Have Universities"[1]

Most of you have probably seen *The Wizard of Oz* (Langley, et. al., 1939). If you're like most people, you may have seen it several times. When I was a child in those long-ago days before cable television, VHS, DVD, and Netflix, the film was shown once a year from 1959 to 1980. Every year we gathered in front of the television as a family. It may surprise you to know that we did that for several years without a color television. You can't imagine how amazing it was to watch the sepia tones of Kansas become the Technicolor vistas of Oz for the first time!

I want to consider the Oz traveling companions as a means of introduction to the university setting. We will look together at The Scarecrow (faculty), The Tin Woodman (student life), The Lion (staff and administration), and Dorothy (students)[2] and consider the journey each is traveling. It may stretch your imagination a bit and, no doubt, cause cries of concern from those within the categories, but it will help you understand some of the dynamics of your university.

For those of you who have never seen it or read the book, here's a bare-bones summary. Dorothy Gale, a frustrated teenage girl, and her dog, Toto, are carried "over the rainbow" by a tornado. When they land, they find

1. *The Wizard of Oz*, said by the Wizard of Oz.

2. There really isn't a parallel for the Wizard in the university itself. I could argue that external groups like accrediting agencies could fit but that's outside our primary focus. Whenever I talk about the Wizard of Oz analogy, people ask what Toto represents. I have absolutely no idea but remain open to suggestions!

49

themselves in the Land of Oz: a magical place of witches, talking animals, Flying Monkeys, and Munchkins. From the beginning, Dorothy wants to know how to get home. She is told to "follow the yellow brick road" to find the Wizard of Oz, the only person thought to have the power to get her home. In her arrival, she lands on the Wicked Witch of the East and kills her, much to the furor of the Witch's sister, the Wicked Witch of the West. Dorothy inherits the East Witch's Ruby Slippers, upsetting West even more. Dorothy sets off on her journey to the Wizard and is soon joined by a Scarecrow, a Tin Woodman, and a Cowardly Lion. Together they go to the Wizard, confront the Witch, and have many adventures. All of the travellers have something special they want to ask of the Wizard. The Scarecrow wants a Brain, the Tin Woodman wants a Heart, and the Cowardly Lion wants Courage. After their harrowing journey, they get what they were looking for and Dorothy finds herself back home.

At least that was Frank Baum's original story (Baum & Denslow, 1900). In recent years, Gregory Maguire has written a series of books, starting with *Wicked*, which was made into a hit Broadway show. Maguire tells the story about Ephelba (we know her as the Wicked Witch of the West), who wasn't a Witch at all, and how she was caught up in the political intrigues of Oz.[3]

Much of the dialogue in *The Wizard of Oz* is familiar, even if you haven't seen the movie. You may know about "*The Lollipop Guild*" that some of the Munchkins belong to. You've probably heard the Witch say, "*I'll get you, my pretty, and your little dog too!*" Or you may recognize Dorothy's phrase, "*There's no place like home,*" which she repeats in order to eventually get back to Kansas.

One of the most repeated lines from the film comes when the group visits the Wizard. While they are looking at the "Great and Powerful Wizard" with flames around his giant head, Toto finds a man running the controls. The Wizard says, "*Pay no attention to the man behind the curtain!*"

For much of our lives, the systems that we are a part of also tell us not to look beneath the surface understandings. We saw this in the bureaucratic, "next steps" approach to college choice. It takes some careful thought to get behind the curtain and glimpse what's really going on.

I want to use some of the characters from *The Wizard of Oz* to examine the nature of the Christian university you've joined. I'm not trying to uncover frauds (the Wizard said he was "*a good man, just a very bad*

---

3. How we tell a story matters to all the characters and to the reader!

Wizard") but to understand the dynamics of how the various pieces of the community fit together and where natural tensions exist.

Acknowledging that differing positions and perspectives exist in higher education does not inevitably lead to conflict (although conflict may be experienced temporarily—more on this in future chapters). In fact, it is the dialogue between the various segments of the community that a college, on its good days, does best.

It is overly simplistic to talk of the generic faculty member, student life professional, or president. We are each unique individuals with the histories, challenges, skills, talents, foibles, insecurities, and fears that help define our sense of self.

And yet there is value in generalization. While the generality or description of a category may not fit every person within it, the commonalities that exist can differentiate one category from another. In this sense, it makes sense to treat the faculty members, student life professionals, staff members or administrators, and students as four separate groups coexisting as constituent parts of the academic setting. If we understand these different roles, we have a better sense of how they combine their efforts for the good of the overall community.

The Scarecrow: Faculty

Dorothy comes upon the Scarecrow as she is carefully following the Yellow Brick Road. She comes across an intersection and wonders which way to turn (since the road goes both directions). The Scarecrow is hanging on a post surrounded by crows, being unable to do the one job for which he was created. He is just not very frightening to the average crow. He immediately offers Dorothy assistance in solving her problem. He tells her what others have done before her. He gives some advice, all the while admitting how much better he would be "*if he only had a brain.*"

For not having a brain, the Scarecrow actually knows a lot. In his song and dance, he makes reference to significant figures like Abraham Lincoln. He has collected information, stored it away, and recalls it as appropriate. He's even the mastermind behind the plan to disguise the travelers as Winkies (the guards at the witch's castle). But he really wants a brain, so that he can be recognized for his deep wisdom and superior knowledge. He agrees to accompany Dorothy to find the Wizard and make his request in person. When he finally meets the Wizard he is told of the wisdom he already demonstrated. He is reminded of his problem-solving abilities and how he had applied those when the travelers were in danger.

The Wizard tells the Scarecrow all the bright things he has done and that he lacked but one thing: a diploma (Why College Reason #2). His knowledge and learning needed to be authenticated by some other organization. Someone had to officially recognize his braininess. So the Wizard gives him a diploma.

The only time the Scarecrow acts superior to others is when he makes his first proclamation after the diploma is granted. His voice deepens and he sounds very "*professorial*" as he proclaims, "*The sum of the square roots of any two sides of a isosceles triangle is equal to the square root of the remaining side.*" He is now certain of his intelligence, even though it is wrong.[4]

The Scarecrow provides a model for examining the life and role of a college professor. It is helpful to begin with an examination of what attracts someone to the vocation of college professor.

Each professor has her own story, but some generalizations are possible for most faculty members. First, it is safe to argue that those persons who consider the profession feel quite comfortable within the academic environment. They enjoy the disciplines of reading and writing. For aspiring professors, the world of ideas presents an ongoing and exciting challenge (in fact, a manual activity in the physical realm, like working on a car, may seem impossible.) When faculty members were students, they likely exhibited a strong sense of intrinsic motivation, an ability to focus on what was important, and a reasonable sense of time management. In other words, faculty members learned how to navigate the landscape of higher education early on in their college career.

Sometimes this ease at navigation results in a sense of frustration with those who don't share that inside knowledge. I distinctly remember a hallway conversation with faculty colleagues a number of years ago. It happened that a number of students had volunteered to serve as caddies for an alumni golf tournament the weekend before finals week. My faculty friends couldn't understand how these students could not recognize what their proper priorities were. They commented, "*We never would have put anything above our studies when we were in college.*" I responded, "*Yes, but you have to recognize that you were never **normal** students!*"

4. The Pythagorean Theorem actually says that the sum of *the squares of* the sides of a right triangle is equal to the square of the hypotenuse.

Understanding the path faculty members took to get where they are is key to effectively interacting with them. The more you grasp how they think, the more effective your learning will be.

Being good at the *"academic game"* is not sufficient to prepare someone for college teaching. A more important dynamic is commonly at work. Most of the faculty members I have known were *captured* by their subject matter somewhere during the course of their studies. In other words, something about the subject matter itself was intriguing, it underscored questions the individual had considered for a long time, or raised issues that simply couldn't be escaped.

When I went from high school to college, American society had been through a number of serious transitions. During my adolescent and young adult years, I was confronted by a war in Southeast Asia, race riots in America's cities, the assassinations of Bobby Kennedy and Martin Luther King Jr., a major prison riot, and the resignation of a president. For me, these events raised powerful questions regarding the nature of justice, social order, individual freedom, and community standards. I was also dealing with issues of identity related to the divorce of my parents and my struggles for acceptance in high school.

When I began to study sociology, I found that sociologists were also asking the kinds of questions that I had struggled with. The sociological approach revolves around changes in structure, both small (the individual) and large (society as a whole). In many ways, when I began the serious study of sociology, I found a home.

Parker Palmer tells a story of another faculty member captured by her field. Barbara McClintock was a Nobel-prize-winning-biologist. During her career, she seemed to have a passion for genetics that was hard to explain. According to her biographer, Evelyn Fox Keller, what made Barbara McClintock's work so special was that she "loved" the corn:

> "What enabled McClintock to see further and deeper into the mysteries of genetics than her colleagues?" McClintock's answer, Keller tells us, is simple: "Over and over again she tells us one must have the time to look, the patience to 'hear what the material has to say to you,' the openness to 'let it come to you.' Above all, one must have 'a feeling for the organism.'" (quoted in [Palmer, 1998]: p. 55)

It would be an overstatement to suggest that this explanation describes every college professor a student will ever encounter. I have known those people who entered college teaching because they happened into it or because it was the only way they could pursue a research career. A few professors enjoy the flexibility of their schedule or the joys of summer projects, but these are few and far between. Most faculty members would agree that we teach for free and get paid to grade papers and go to committee meetings. The joy of introducing our personal passion to new groups of students each semester is incredibly fulfilling.

Not unlike the Scarecrow when he begins down the Yellow Brick Road, most faculty members stumble into the passion of their lives somewhere during their college experience. Following that passion introduces the challenges of graduate school because the only way to college teaching is through the gateway of advanced degrees.

The rigors of graduate school force the individual to move from general content to specific content, from passion for the subject to definitions, methods, and learning of the giants of the discipline. Graduate school requires pushing well beyond comfortable levels in workload and demands that one move forward even if mastering everything seems an impossible task. In fact, one of the dangers of graduate school is that the experience may remove everything that was considered "*fun*" about the original subject.

There are specific dynamics to graduate education. Not only do expectations drastically increase, but so does the level of criticism. Much of graduate education relies on a seminar format where students evaluate each other's work; individuals quickly learn to be critical of the work of others. One learns to identify schools of thought, pet arguments, disciplinary "*heroes*," and to provide rational alternatives to those viewpoints.

But one cannot be an expert in everything. Graduate programs are complex places involving a wide variety of specializations. This narrowness of specialization must be avoided when one joins a liberal arts university. There a faculty member is valued as a generalist more than a specialist. Being a generalist is a daunting experience because one is consistently drawn into areas where one is not an expert while maintaining personal confidence and the trust of students.

There is another aspect of graduate education that shapes a faculty member: the dissertation. Even though the specifics of the doctoral dissertation varies by disciplinary area, it generally requires one to develop a unique area of exploration, explore existing academic literature, carefully analyze the study in question, draw general conclusions, and raise questions about how the discipline is enhanced as a result. It is a process of intense personal focus, deep frustration, occasional excitement, and long hours (days, weeks, months, or years) of writing and editing.

In writing my own dissertation, two emotions stayed with me at all times. First, I was excited about the project and believed it had something important to say to sociologists. Second, I didn't want anyone to read it because I didn't want to invite criticism of my arguments, especially when I'd invested that much time.[5]

With the writing project over, the fun begins. Depending upon the school and the discipline, there may be numerous readers with varied opinions. Some have specific ideas about what should be added to make a better project and each often has his or her preferred style of argument. Often the amount of time spent editing to meet the demands of the committee far exceeds the time taken to write the first full draft. The challenge is to rewrite without losing one's way and having the project become someone else's.

The final step in the process is the dissertation defense. The candidate sits down with the committee to answer questions about anything in the book-length document. "Why is this argument stated as it is on page 234?" "Why wasn't the material of so-and-so included in the discussion in the middle of chapter four?" "How does one reconcile these conclusions with those made in this paper published just last week?"

For many, the dominant emotion of the dissertation defense is regret that one began in the first place. Instead the process becomes one of survival. Most faculty members can recite horror stories of dissertation experiences gone terribly wrong. They recount how friends or acquaintances had such a horrible situation that they walked away, never to finish. The stereotype of the cab driver or fast food server who almost finished the doctorate (known professionally as ABD—*"all but dissertation"* [6]) speaks to this final hurdle.

Why is this hurdle significant? It matters so much to faculty because it speaks of passion for the subject, the development of careful (or at least effective) work habits, and the persistence to see it through. All of us who have been through the process know those who didn't have *"what it takes."* These individuals (who may have been much brighter than any of us) didn't see how they could maintain their focus through the entire process, and they quit school somewhere along the way.

---

5. A combination of emotions that regularly resurfaced in the writing of this book!

6. Refers to someone who completed all required coursework but hasn't finished the dissertation.

A few pages ago, I introduced my faculty friends who complained about the alumni golf tournament. At the time, I was being less than sympathetic to their way of viewing the world (maybe because I wasn't a good student at first). But looking through the lens of personal passion for the subject material, the survival of the rigors of graduate school, and the deep conviction of the dissertation, I have to grant them their indignation. From the time they were students themselves, they have wrapped their identity around their disciplinary material. It spoke to them when they were in graduate school and nurtured them through the dissertation phase.

The students who skipped class to be caddies inadvertently denied the personal identity of the faculty members. Their choice worked to dismiss the faculty members' own story. Taking such an easy approach to their studies seemed to suggest that the faculty members' commitments had been excessive, silly, and futile.

Like the Scarecrow in Oz, faculty members celebrate the value of the brain. They want to encourage students to think deeply, ask questions they would rather not confront (remember Peter's vision in chapter 1?), and develop a personal passion for the material. Faculty members often do act like their class is the most important of all in the curriculum because to them it must be so. If only everyone else could see the value of learning, recognize the power of a developed mind, and experience the driving passion of ideas. While they would never use these exact words, when faculty members relate to the other segments of the Christian university they seem to exclaim that the entire process would work better if those other folks *"only had a brain."*

The Tin Woodman: Student Life/Residence Life/Athletics

As Dorothy and the Scarecrow travel through the Enchanted Forest on their way to see the Wizard, they come across a figure standing by the side of the road. While the movie doesn't give details on how he got there, the books do. The Tin Woodman was once a Human Woodman who was in love with a local girl. To keep him away from the girl, the Witch enchanted his axe so that it cut off his limbs. Each time he lost a limb, the tinsmith made him an artificial one. But the axe, still enchanted, kept chopping and the Woodman kept replacing body parts. Eventually, he lost all his limbs. But the Tinsmith left him without the one thing most important to him: a heart.

He wanted to feel compassion. He wanted to connect deeply with others and be able to feel what they felt. As he says in the song, *"I'd be tender, I'd be gentle, I'd be kind and sentimental . . ."* When he finally gets to the Wizard, he receives a testimonial[7] in honor of his compassion for others. Just like the Scarecrow, he didn't really need the testimonial because he had already expressed deep emotion throughout and placed a higher value on others than himself. As Dorothy is preparing to leave Oz, the Tin Woodman says, *"I know I must have a heart because I can feel it breaking."*

Ernest Boyer reminded us of the seventy hours a week students spend in what we think of as the "co-curriculum." Staff members who give themselves to student activities, residence life, campus ministry, career development, and athletics do so because they want to engage in the lives of the students attending the college. Compassion is at the center of their world.

Student development personnel recognize that one of the most important things happening to you during your college years is a development of your individual sense of voice. As we have already discussed, college is a time of great transition where students set goals and establish habits that say a great deal about their future development. To manage this transition successfully, you need a sense of personal direction, confidence, calling, and drive. In other words, even while student development staff are motivated by compassion and empathy, they identify the development of *your* heart as their most critical task. To a great extent, they do that by connecting their heart to yours.

Each student is working through a process of *"meaning making[8],"* in which events of life become the raw materials for identifying your unique voice. Academic classes, student ministry opportunities, lunch with a professor, family relationships, current events, dating and romance, chapel, work experiences, and textbooks act like jigsaw puzzle pieces from which you assemble a meaningful picture.

Putting the puzzle together is complicated; no one really knows what the final picture ought to be. It is as if you were putting together a 1,000-piece puzzle of a landscape, but without the box lid.

---

7. I've always thought this was the lamest of the Wizard's gifts. A ribbon given to *"good deed doers"* is not what motivates folks like the Tin Woodman. In fact, watching the movie while writing this lets me know that the Tin Woodman gets the short stick throughout. His song is shortest. He contributes but doesn't lead. In short, he seems to be a nearly extraneous member of the team. It's really too bad. Heart is really important!

8. Chapter 7 explores meaning making in depth.

The focus on meaning-making and character development requires a significant amount of trial and error followed by reflection. This is a difficult task filled with the possibility for mistake, confusion, and uncertainty. It's sometimes hard to figure out precisely what worked and why.

Thus, the concept of _mentor_ is one of the most important in student development work. Sharon Daloz Parks provides an overview of the richness of this concept:

> _Mentor_ is a venerable term, grounded in Homer's _Odyssey_ and laden with expectations of a tradition of guiding wisdom. It has been popularly captured in the figures of Obi-Wan Kenobi and Yoda in George Lucas's _Star Wars_ film trilogy . . .
>
> Indeed, good mentors help to anchor the promise of the future. As young adults are beginning to think critically about self and world, mentors give them crucial forms of recognition, support, and challenge. There is more. Mentors care about your soul. Whatever the immediate challenge or subject matter, good mentors know that all knowledge has a moral dimension, and learning that matters is ultimately a spiritual, transforming activity, intimately linked with the whole of life. (2000, p. 127–28)

Mentors feel a deep sense of responsibility for those students under their care. It is interesting that Parks refers to the relationship between either Obi-Wan Kenobi or Yoda with Luke Skywalker as her prototypical example of a mentor. This opens an interesting contrast between the first Star Wars trilogy and the second trilogy of prequels. One of the themes of the more recent films in the Star Wars franchise explores how Obi-Wan's attempt to mentor the young, volatile Anakin Skywalker results in failure and births the powerful and heartless Darth Vader. If mentoring Luke provides the ideal relationship, the failure to develop Anakin underscores the fear of anyone in a mentoring relationship. The joy of seeing an uncertain life become disciplined, purposed, and hopeful is a rewarding thing for a mentor. The fear of seeing that life go awry and pursue its own path, like the Prodigal Son, for example, is a source of haunting doubt.

That there is but a narrow line between joyful success and fearful loss is why student development folks so highly prize one-on-one relationships with students. They are keenly aware of the possible impact of their actions on those students with whom they interact. I once heard a staff member express deep concern over a policy decision by referring to the admonition in Matthew 18:6 that one who causes a child to stumble should have a millstone tied around his neck and dropped into the sea. In the context of the situation I thought this was a misuse of the scriptural reference (students are not little children), but the sentiment did underscore the significance we have on student lives.

For student development personnel, the possibility of impacting the lives of others around them is a singular motivation. Whether working with roommate relationships in a residence hall, assisting a student in considering career options, helping a student cope with family issues in a counseling setting, improving the basketball skills of the freshman point guard, or even working through a disciplinary issue, they are investing in your process of learning through that specific situation.[9] They draw purpose in their hopes and prayers for your future course of action beyond the university years.

While not true of all student development personnel, it is safe to argue that the majority of them entered the field because they developed an awareness of how their own life was shaped by mentors. Significant individuals stepped into their lives at critical moments. For the Tin Woodman, it was a kindly doctor who took pity on him and fixed him up. Looking back, student life staff acknowledge and honor those who played such a crucial role in their own development. They may even have an awareness of where they would be today if not for the influence of that other person. With some exceptions, student development folks do their work because someone truly believed in them. It's not uncommon to hear one say, "*I never thought I would do this until [insert mentor's name] called me into the office one day.*"

As I reflect on people I have known in the student development arena, similarities emerge in their journeys into this vocation. A work-study job in the admissions department opens up a post-college job. The resident assistant moves into an eventual resident director role. The resident director becomes director of career planning. The student assistant on the soccer team becomes assistant coach, then head coach, then athletic director. The student government president eventually becomes director of student activities.

Career paths such as these may not happen within a single institution. It may be necessary to move around to pursue such opportunities. Student development folks may not have really set out to do their work as a career goal, but they found they were good, the work was fulfilling, and it spoke to their heart.

9. We'll return to this in chapter 8.

They believe in paying things forward: they invest in your life because someone invested in theirs. This is how they repay the kindness within God's economy. They mentor students because someone else effectively mentored them.

Relationships between students and mentors may be closer in those instances where people share common backgrounds and goals. These mentoring relationships will be deep and personal. Alternatively, differing life experiences may result in continual misunderstandings in the meaning-making process.

Another factor impacting the mentoring relationship is the life stage the college student occupies. We again come back to the importance of the Second Big Transition from home to college and from control to independence. As we saw in the previous chapter, as a new student in college you may experience a degree of exploration. Sometimes even well-intentioned, properly motivated, Christian college students like you engage in behaviors that can only be characterized as stupid and careless. The mentor's relationship with you may change over time as part of motivating you to grow and take responsibility. The nature of trust may move from being implicit to explicit as contract relationships (agreements as to behavior) are added to personal relationships (where you are defined only by who you are).

Another aspect of the mentoring relationship deserves special mention. Just as the behavior of the student may affect the ongoing nature of the relationship, the mentor's behavior is also under continual scrutiny. A mentor is expected to be blameless, purposeful, spiritual, compassionate, and fair. When a mentor fails to be one of these things, the trusting nature of the relationship is jeopardized. This is a special hazard for student development personnel. On the one hand, they tend to be committed to a consistent philosophy that guides their behaviors. On the other hand, their commitment to mentorship recognizes that each individual situation is different and should be treated accordingly.

The student development person stands in a precarious position between being fair to all and recognizing your uniqueness. This creates a tension within the mentor to be both consistent and responsive at the same time. Managing that tension successfully calls for the student development person to continually monitor motivation, reaction, intent, balance, and compassion.

This is why the development of heart is so important to people working in the co-curriculum. Like the Tin Woodman, they strive to *feel* their way through their situation. They know they have succeeded when they review the end of the mentoring relationship at a commencement ceremony or when the student is ready to leave the college.

Even though student development folks know that the biology professor and the financial aid counselor love the students, they have a tendency to think that they are the ones that *truly* care for the students. Their developed sense of heart feeds their hope to see you develop a heart for others in your own life.

The Lion: Staff and Administration

As Dorothy, the Scarecrow, and the Tin Woodman move on toward the Emerald City, they come into a wooded area where a Lion confronts them. Their first response is panic and fear in the face of such a powerful animal. Upon closer examination, they discover that the Lion is not quite as fearsome as he first appears.

The Lion lacks courage. He spends his time running through the cover of the forest periodically scaring other animals (he goes after Toto) but doesn't have the ability to lead his kingdom. In his verse of *"If I Only Had . . ."* he says he lacks nerve. He says he's a "dandy lion." Naturally, he joins the company as they travel to Oz, where he will ask the Wizard for courage.

When they get to Oz, the Lion sings another song about what he'd do if he were *"King of the Forest."* The song reflects his dreams of personal respect in the midst of a peaceable kingdom. He wants to be seen as one who made a difference in the lives of others. His perfect world would be one in which he was esteemed and trusted because of his power, although he'd rarely use it.

It's a long jump from the Cowardly Lion to Aslan in the Narnia chronicles. But the contrast between them is instructive. You probably know the lines from *The Lion, the Witch, and the Wardrobe*: Mr. Beaver says, *"Of course he isn't safe. But he's good."*[10] I think Mr. Beaver says what the Cowardly Lion hopes people would say about him.

The Lion represents that segment of the college that is focused on the daily life and future dreams of the college community. There are employees concerned with keeping the campus looking nice. Others make sure

---

10. I'm well aware that Lewis and many readers see Aslan as an allegory of God. I'm not equating the Cowardly Lion or administrators with God. It's just a wonderful statement of what the Cowardly Lion is saying life would be like if he were King.

supplies are ordered, paid for, and accounted for. Still others (like the president) are given the task of overseeing all segments of the college to see that its component parts work together smoothly and that the college is preparing for the demands of the future. Like the Lion in the forest, students or parents rarely see much of what these people do. There is an awareness that they are working but there is certainly less clarity about what they do than a history professor or the basketball coach.

The administrative staff is similar to the Lion in being relatively invisible, but a far more important factor exists. Much of the work done by folks in this segment of college life is based on daily, incremental process. Forms must be reconciled, meetings attended, and personnel evaluations conducted. A focus on such detail makes it difficult to stay focused on the "*big picture.*" It is hard to worry about improving the college for the future when one is caught up in the minutiae of today's task or the crisis of one student's problem.

Much has been written in recent years about how to improve the operation of organizations like colleges. Issues we explored in the second chapter are rehashed in the popular media. Hardly a week goes by without commentators, consultants, and politicians giving their answers for what universities should do.

What keeps administrators and staff members from exhibiting courage? Change can be personally difficult. It disrupts the comfortable patterns of an organizational system. When an administrator prompts change, it makes life very uncomfortable for the students, faculty members, and student development personnel involved. These affected folks are unlikely to stay silent about their newfound discomfort. Given the relatively high priority on maintaining interpersonal relationships in a university setting, change comes at a high cost.

Two other thoughts about courage need to be explored. First, courage requires a commitment to the success of the organization over the long run and not just the short run. In some ways, an administrator must be focused on the university your children will attend more than on the one you attend. The future must be anticipated if the past practices are not simply to be repeated year after year. In the absence of courage, administrators may be tempted to look back to the university your parents attended. Courage involves moving forward and never backward.

Secondly, concern over personal courage has a parallel in my expectations for everyone in the university. Earlier I described how faculty put a priority on the development of a brain and student development personnel put a priority on the development of heart. When they exhibit courage, they must demonstrate responsible behaviors. This sense of responsibility means that they have recognized the contribution they make to the overall progress of the institution, even if it comes at personal cost.

Students should be concerned about pre-registration not just to get their desired classes but to allow the institution to properly project class needs. Faculty members rework favorite classes because doing so strengthens the entire curriculum, even when it causes more work for them. All members of the community recognize that changes in program or policy, even if they are hard to swallow, are recommended to bring about a better, stronger community in the future. Future-oriented policy assumes that the individual recommending the changes has also made the difficult personal changes that accompany institutional change. If the organizational change is coming as a result of positional power (*"because I'm in charge and I said that's how it will be"*), it is hard to see any real institutional change except that which comes from coercion.

When the no-longer-Cowardly Lion meets the Wizard, he is given a medal in honor of his bravery in the face of wicked witches. He engaged in appropriate actions in defense of those he cared about. In so doing, he discovered that the most important changes took place within his sense of self. Confronting who he was meant to be required the greatest courage of all. Once the Lion had managed that internal obstacle, a wicked witch didn't seem so bad.

Dorothy: Students

We've just spent two chapters looking at the shape of your world, so this part of my allegory can be brief. I want to look at it because it underscores some earlier themes.

What Dorothy desires above all is *"home."* She feels lost and cut off. What would make her fulfilled is to have a place where she belongs. Most students are searching for something similar. It's not a perfect match because Dorothy is too young to be out on her own. She wants life back on the farm as she remembered it.

Dorothy's time in Oz is a hiatus from her normal (black and white) life. She is physically removed from her circumstances and from the time she arrives in Oz she is seeking to get back to Kansas. Oz, therefore, isn't her real home. Notice that this isn't the case for anyone else she meets on her journey with the exception of the Wizard. As strange as Munchkins, talking Scarecrows, and witches (both wicked and good) seem to Dorothy, they are a regular part of life for "native" Ozians.

It is easy for students to assume that college is something they are doing between leaving home after high school and getting their first adult job. The command to simply "Follow the Yellow Brick Road" suggests that the really important stuff happens when you get to the Wizard in Emerald City (commencement). Too many students spend their time either looking back to what was left behind or anticipating what might be coming in the future. Little time is spent appreciating the journey being traveled.

A pair of scenes at the movie's end speaks to this issue. The first happens just before Dorothy clicks the Ruby Slippers together while repeating, "*There's no place like home.*" Glinda the Good Witch asks Dorothy about the lesson she has learned. Consider the power of Dorothy's answer:

> I think that it wasn't enough to want to see Uncle Henry and Aunt Em. If I ever go looking for my heart's desire again, I won't look any further than my own backyard. Because if it wasn't there, I never really lost it to begin with.

Dorothy learned that she should find her sense of "*home*" within herself. It is a search for her unique identity. As she says, if she can't find it even if she's at the farm in Kansas she won't find it in the wonderful Land of Oz.

The second scene occurs right before the credits roll. Dorothy is lying on her bed and everyone has gathered around to see if she's okay. When everyone thinks she's had a vivid dream, with that dismissive tone adults use with young people, Dorothy retorts:

> This was a real truly live place. Some of it wasn't very nice, but most of it was beautiful.

Dorothy recognizes that everything she experienced was part of her learning. She can't take the Munchkins without the Flying Monkeys. She can't get to the Emerald City without dealing with the temptation of the poppy field (with Glinda's help). All of it is part of the real truly live place.

We learn another lesson about students by looking at Dorothy: She believes that the solution to all her problems lies in what the Wizard does. He must be able to provide the answers she seeks. After all, he is Oz, the Great and Powerful. None of the travellers really know anything about the Wizard, but they assume that he can solve their problems. If those solutions aren't immediately forthcoming, then maybe the Wizard is just a nice misguided man.

Students sometimes believe that the solutions to their life issues are a direct result of the actions of a faculty advisor, key professor in a required class, residence hall director, or college president. If that person would exercise personal gifts and demonstrate the power of the position, the student would be individually whole, academically adept, and fully employable in a fulfilling job. If those things don't happen, the Wizard wasn't much of a Wizard after all.

This projection of personal responsibility is a challenge for students. The sooner they come to terms with their own ability to produce change within themselves, the more meaningful the college experience will be. If there is one critical realization that changed my college story from failure to success, it was learning that it was up to me. Mentors and professors could provide me with perspective, but it was up to me to make the necessary adjustments in attitudes and habits.

Dorothy's story, finally, has to do with the way the four travelers (plus Toto) begin to form a community.[11] Dorothy directly impacts the lives of the Scarecrow, the Tin Woodman, and the Lion. Each of them decides to go with her to Emerald City because of her optimism and the depth of her belief. Because of their commitment to each other, they develop the skills and attributes they most desired in life. These proved to be life-saving on several occasions.

I have already spent time on the passive nature of much of American education. Students are socialized into believing that their role is to simply jump through the required hoops with minimal fuss. Too often, they are seen as cogs in some larger machine simply performing the role expected of them.

Like Dorothy on the road with the others, students can fundamentally alter the nature of a student activity, an athletic team, or a classroom. The level of enthusiasm they bring, the amount of personal change they are willing to risk, and the degree to which they enter into partnership with a professor directly impacts the quality of the education they receive. This is an awesome power, one that can be used to inhibit the educational work going on or one that can greatly enhance education well beyond anyone's plans.

11. A process we will explore in depth in chapter 6.

Dorothy's life impacted the others. She becomes responsible for Aunt Em's health. She worries if she has gotten her friends into great danger. She even feels sorry for melting the wicked witch. As we have already seen, we're all part of each other's story. This brings great joy and great responsibility.

Here, then, are the lessons that can be drawn from considering the component parts of the Christian university through the lenses provided by *The Wizard of Oz*. Most importantly, each segment of the community holds a slightly different perspective on the values defining the community as a whole. These perspectives are not exclusive, however. Faculty members are aware that you need to develop heart, and administrators are concerned with courage. Student development workers will be the first to recognize that the college is primarily an academic community and that you develop your sense of self within the context of classes in the pursuit of learning.

Second, all segments of the community hold to the view that your wholeness is of utmost value. Faculty members, staff members, student development folks, the president, and the student government desire that you, during your time in the university, develop a balance of brain, heart, courage, and identity.

Our goal is the self-construction of whole beings that express the image of God in their own personal sense of what that means. To the extent that this is achieved, it is also reflected in the overall operation of the Christian university itself. A community focused on your wholeness and uniqueness will itself reflect its own communal sense of wholeness and uniqueness. If you are challenged to be authentic, the community will be seen as authentic. Stating this in the negative, a community that is not committed to balance in the lives of individuals, that supports only particular aspects of the self (whether brain or heart or courage) will itself be a broken community riddled with a sense of falseness. It will be like a Wizard projecting images on a big screen while hiding behind a curtain.

Finally, while it may be useful to think of broad categories within the Christian university, the categories provide a handle that make it easier to describe the reality we see. However, the categories I have described fall away when one looks instead at a community consisting of a group of committed individuals. Earlier, I described the life events that made sociology attractive to me. My experiences are different from my faculty colleagues, even in sociology. The experience of the Dean of Students is different from the person in charge of housing. Professionally, being a sociologist or a

Dean of Students is part of the internal identity of an individual, but the role does not in itself determine the identity. It is one part among many.

Communities like Christian universities must remain dependent upon individuals knowing how to tell their stories clearly, how to listen to one another, and how to be attentive to the Holy Spirit as bridges are built between speaker and listener. Appreciating the uniqueness of each individual as a created being is one more aspect in understanding the dynamics of the Christian higher education.

This section was kind of a enlightenment on the christian university, and how it works.

5

Why Is Christian Higher Education Christian?

We saw earlier how Christian Smith and his colleagues, exploring the religious commitments of eighteen to twenty-three year olds in *Souls in Transition* (C. Smith, 2009), described three categories of unbelief and three categories of Christian belief. Students ranged from being Committed Traditionalists to Selective Adherents to Spiritually Open. It is likely, when compared to emerging adults generally, to find a higher percentage of Christian university students in the first group. As we've also seen, some of those students picked the Christian university because it has an inviting atmosphere for believers (chapel, Christian faculty and staff, lessened pressures from alcohol).

A question needs to be asked: Can we think of Christian higher education without simply seeing it as part of the broader evangelical subculture? The evangelical community has tended to create "parallel universes" that enable individual behaviors within safe environments. We can go to bookstores and buy "Christian fiction," go to "Christian music" concerts, and even find places with "Christian Aerobics" (where you exercise only to Christian music). There has to be more to our task than only seeing "Christian university" as but another example of special interest.

Sociologists and psychologists have long examined the distinctions we make between in-groups and out-groups within society. We root for our team/tribe and look with suspicion toward other teams/tribes. We talk to each other about how our team is great ("we're number one") regardless of our actual performance record ("we're tied for fourth"). We wonder how "they" can believe what they believe. If only "they" were as enlightened as "we" are. Such tribalism has contributed to a failure of civil discourse[1] and, on a national scale, the challenges of effective government.

My eyes were opened to the in-group biases a few years ago when I heard Reggie McNeal speak at a church convention. Reggie is a church insider; a Southern Baptist from South Carolina, he has invested his life in ministry and ministry preparation. His speech, drawing from his book *The Present Future* (2003), was intended to shake up a complacent group of church leaders. It did— it shook me to my bones.

McNeal argued that we've been church-focused rather than mission-focused. In other words, we've been worried about how to get people to join "our team" rather than figuring out how to meet people where they are. That internal church focus reflects exactly what the Barna folks saw as the things that kept young people from church (in chapter 3) or pushed them away. It's the message behind Jeff Bethke's poem.

James Davidson Hunter has been informing academics about evangelicalism for decades. In the early 1980s he wrote *American Evangelicalism* (Hunter, 1983) which provided a solid sociological introduction to the evangelical movement. I've always found the subtitle to be particularly intriguing: Conservative Religion and the Quandary of Modernity. The modern world—characterized by rationality, pluralism of thought, and dialogue[2]—presents particular challenges to people of faith. They want to connect with the culture, but doing so risks accommodating the Christian message.

In his most recent work, *To Change the World* (2010), Hunter continues an exploration of the same challenges nearly thirty years later. He suggests that there are three approaches the church has used to engage "the world": Defensive Against, Relevance to, and Purity From.

The first option sees the surrounding culture as a threat that must be constantly engaged. Seeing the world as increasingly secular, a spirit of distrust develops. Evangelicals want to reach out to the unchurched but are constantly on guard against threat. The annual concern about a "War on Christmas" provides an extreme version of this defensive stance.

---

1. Civil Discourse addresses how we engage in discussion with others in ways that are respectful, informed, and seeking to achieve some form of consensus.

2. Since the Enlightenment period, we have believed that rational argument supported by empirical evidence was the key to knowledge. Faith has a hard time meeting such a standard.

The second option, Relevance, is an attempt to accommodate the larger society. This has been the preferred strategy of much of mainline religion during the twentieth century. It also characterizes some segments of the "emergent church" as younger evangelicals attempt to find ways of engaging the broader culture without the "negative" rhetoric that the Barna studies found so inflammatory. Recent denominational debates on homosexuality by Episcopalians, Presbyterians, and Methodists (to name just three) reflect the tensions between the first two options within Christianity. Those members favoring Relevance want the church to lead on issues of marriage equality. Others argue that the church must Defend against social change. This has led to separation movements within the Episcopal Church.

The Purity From response maintains a separatist stance that characterized religious groups from the late nineteenth and early twentieth centuries. Of course, it can still be seen in Amish and some Mennonite communities, as well as in twenty-something, intentional Christian living communities in urban settings. Most Christian universities were founded with such a stance in mind. It's not surprising that many Christian universities are located far from big cities!

Rather than these three stances, Hunter suggests a better way: Faithful Presence. He describes this approach:

> Whether within the community of believers or among those outside the church, we imitate our creator and redeemer; we pursue each other, identify with each other, and direct our lives toward the flourishing of each other through sacrificial love. (p. 244)

Faithful Presence involves risk. It resists the temptation to create enclaves that look suspiciously at those who are outside "the Christian bubble." It means we engage those around us, within the community and outside. When the Christian university attempts such risky engagement, it will experience pushback from those folks (pastors, parents, trustees, and alumni) operating within the first three stances. When we add our earlier recognition that you are in the midst of a huge personal and social transition from home to the world beyond college, the risks become not just individual but institutional as well. Your Christian university experience should model Faithful Presence while still allowing you the room for being an emerging adult.

How do we manage that risk? We must have an understanding of our work that is deeply grounded in our understandings of the work of the Trinity. We have to grab hold of a rich understanding of our theological assumptions and what those suggest for us. Understanding theological frameworks allow us to engage the broader world for the Kingdom without falling into either defensiveness or simple relevance.

Christian colleges and universities have long promoted the fact that they were "Christ-centered." This was to suggest that they were different from schools historically related to religious bodies (e.g., Harvard and Yale) that now lack vibrant faith commitments. Attempting to draw out those distinctions, Christian university mission statements are ripe with such language.

The comparison between the secular school and the Christian college runs throughout the history of the Christian college movement. Even as Christian colleges have developed into the quality-accredited institutions they are today, the steps along the journey seem to require a sideways glance at what our secular colleagues are up to.

The Christian colleges in the last half of the twentieth century were different from the schools that prepared ministers from which many arose. As the colleges pursued regional accreditation, it was necessary to find faculty members who held advanced degrees and who specialized in particular subjects. However, this increasing professionalization of the college still required a solid Christian component. It was important for the faculty members to be professing Christians. Many institutions established specific faith statements that prospective faculty were required to affirm, a practice that continues to this day. To maintain the quality of the holistic component of the Christian college, many colleges clarified specific requirements for chapel attendance and religion courses.

The broadening of mission and expansion of program, to say nothing of the social disruptions faced by higher education institutions in the late 1960s and early 1970s, pushed the Christian colleges to attempt to stake out their particular approach to education. These rapid social changes provided the context into which Arthur Holmes, a recognized professor of philosophy at Wheaton College who has served as a spokesman for Christian higher education for the past thirty years, states the particular role of the Christian college. He had asked: "How could the Christian colleges of the early 1970s respond to the growth, expansion, and increased professionalism (stemming from increased reliance on doctorates and strength of regional accreditation) without risking the mission drift that had characterized historically church-related colleges like Harvard and Yale a century earlier?"

In *The Idea of the Christian College*, Holmes attempted to articulate the specific mission of the Christian college as centering on the integration of faith and learning (Holmes, 1975). To Holmes, assumptions and presuppositions about Scripture and Christian tradition have a legitimate place as part of scholarly preparation and become the key mission for the Christian college. The assumptions and presuppositions change the nature of the educational experience regardless of the subject matter taught. The Council for Christian Colleges and Universities has published books illustrating this approach with titles such as Sociology Through the Eyes of Faith (or Biology . . . or Business . . . or History . . .).

An exploration of faith issues constituted a "blind spot" in the critical thinking commitments of secular academics. For many of them, the worldviews that Holmes wanted to integrate were seen as a combination of anti-intellectual faith on the one hand and modern scientific knowledge on the other. Look at the comments section following a religion story on websites like *The Huffington Post* and you'll see these tensions at play.

We need something more substantial than good slogans that can separate us from supposed others or give us nice phrases we can repeat in chapel. What we must have are theological models that help define not only our expectation but even our sense of daily practice.[3]

Theology and Education

Richard Hughes, Professor of Religion at Messiah College, claims that a school's educational character rests on its theological underpinnings (2001). Hughes explores key ideas in theology and explores possible implications for what one assumes about education.

One theological approach Hughes considers is what we know as the Reformed Tradition. The Reformed approach develops out of the theological perspective of John Calvin. Central to John Calvin's vision is the belief that God is Sovereign—everything is under His control. In Calvin's view, this sovereignty extends to civil society and all of its institutional structures: government, family, and education.

This understanding of control creates a special role for an educational institution to play if it is to maintain God's sovereignty. Hughes explains,

---

3. James Smith's Desiring the Kingdom (2009) is a great attempt at examining "liturgies of practice"

> Educators who rely on this vision seek to place the entire cur-
> riculum—and every course within the curriculum—under the
> sovereignty of God. According to this vision, all learning should
> be Christian in both purpose and orientation. (p. 69)

To insure that learning will be Christian throughout the curriculum, the Reformed model first asserts the existence of a distinct Christian worldview. This worldview must identify the unique presuppositions in Calvinist theology that speak to issues of education. For example, it is taken as a given that humans are not simply maximizing their individual potential but are responding to the will of God. Also, what can be seen is only part of the total reality that exists. These presuppositions shape what you read in a course, the nature of a professor's lectures, and the kind of assignments given.

Although Hughes does not address it directly in his book, the understanding of the Fall of Humankind described in Genesis 3 is a significant piece of this understanding of truth. The choice Adam and Eve made in the Garden of Eden resulted in the fall of all of nature, including our ability to explain nature. Not only did the natural world suffer in the Fall, but our rational capacities were limited as well in our ability to interpret what we see in the world around us. Consider the Apostle Paul's statement that the "*foolishness of God*" surpasses the "*wisdom of the world*" (1 Corinthians 3:19). This approach to understanding God's truth requires belief in a distinctively Christian worldview.

According to Hughes, the tension between the sovereignty of God and the understandings of the world calls forth the specific task of the "*integration of faith and learning.*" This proposition suggests that the task of the Christian college is first to articulate the Christian worldview and then to contrast that worldview with other approaches that do not acknowledge the sovereignty of God. As Hughes observes, such a strategy "provides students with a clearly defined standpoint from which to discriminate between competing perspectives and worldviews" (p. 74). The method for discriminating between worldviews follows a formal, logical, propositional approach of examining the presuppositions of a given understanding in contrast with the Christian Worldview.

The Reformed perspective also maintains a strong concern over the challenges of secularization. As Hughes suggests, "Secularization occurs when there is even one dimension of human life that escapes the sovereignty of God, or when we fail to bring all of reality under the umbrella of a distinctly Christian worldview" (p. 73). Seen in this light, the specific role of Christian higher education is to maintain the sovereignty of God in all of our understandings, in contrast to those in the secular academy. From this perspective, for other colleges to deny the role of God is not just a failure educationally, but threatens the entire possibility of establishing a Kingdom of God within society.

While the Reformed/Integration model has been dominant in Christian universities for several decades, I suggest that it doesn't hold up well in these postmodern times. Jake and Rhonda Jacobsen[4] (Jacobsen, Jacobsen, & Sawatsky, 2004) suggest that there has been a shift in education along with a "larger cultural transformation":

> We have moved away from the clearcut [sic], bilateral, Cold War thinking of the *past to the decentered, multilateral, postmodern orientations of today*. Contemporary ways of thought and life are less concerned with the norms of logic favored by the worldview approach and *much more concerned with the quirky and often unpredictable ways things actually fit together in their local and global environments* . . . Christian scholars will probably need to develop a range of new, less grandiose ways of relating faith and learning that are more attuned to contemporary scholarly practices. (pp. 27–28, emphasis mine)

It's not hard to jump from their critique of worldview approaches to the diversity present in your world. There may well be a segment of the Committed Traditionalists comfortable with worldview arguments. The Selective Adherents and Spiritually Open students seem to be exactly those who are concerned with "the quirky and unpredictable ways things fit together."

Postmodernism is a messy concept, with seemingly as many definitions as authors writing about it. It's no doubt possible to think of postmodernism as still in development as we move away from the "taken-for-granted" assumptions of modernism.

Theologian Thomas Oord provides a helpful categorization of forms of postmodernity (Oord, 2009). Oord distinguishes between deconstructive postmodernism, narrative postmodernism, and oppressive postmodernism. The first assumes that we can't know what words mean so

---

4. The Jacobsens' book is addressed to professors like me, not students like you. We'd need to adjust that last line to talk about "today's students" who need to develop new strategies attuned to "the postmodern world".

shared meaning becomes problematic. Narrative postmodernism, as the name suggests, puts a high premium on one person's story. Because each person's story is different, judgmentalism is a risk. Each person's story is unique which runs the risk of in-group thinking. Oppressive postmodernism calls for liberation on behalf of the dispossessed; often giving special privilege to those who are seen as powerless, even if it takes away from others who enjoyed power in the past. Oord instead calls us to a revisionary postmodernism:

> Revisionary postmodernists accept the project of reconstructing a vision of reality. They seek a story big and adequate enough to include everyone. And yet this grand story promotes diversity and difference. (p. 43)

What we need is a theological grounding more compatible with the postmodern world than the earlier worldview approach of Reformed theology. Such an approach will have theological "handles" that will allow us to embrace the diversity present within Christian universities while avoiding the danger of drifting away from our core mission.

John Welsey's "Method"

I find those handles in the life, work, and thought of John Wesley. Wesley was born in 1703 in England. He represented the established church (Anglican) while also exploring new approaches to expressing Christianity. He was Oxford[5] trained and served as an Oxford fellow (teacher). He had a distinctive experience of affirmation of faith and searched ways for others to experience the same. He read widely with an intriguing way of combining faith and learning. He established a method of group life (which is why we call it "Methodism") that focused on ways for diverse people to support one another in their faith. Wesley's work, according to theologian Howard Snyder, was complex and dynamic:

> Wesley's genius, under God, lay in developing and maintaining a synthesis in doctrine and practice that kept biblical paradoxes paired and powerful. He held together faith and works, doctrine and experience, the individual and the social, the concerns of time

5. Wesley faced his own challenges as a student as one biographer reported: "He worked as hard as ever and did well, though he still castigated himself for idleness. This was probably because he had such a full social life—tennis and billiards, boating and walks, chess and cards, dances, theatre and coffee houses" (Tomkins, 2003, 22).

> and eternity. It is this synthesis that speaks most profoundly to the church today. (1980, p. 143)

Snyder's point about a *"synthesis between doctrine and practice"* is well taken. We will see that the tension between the two is instructive for Christian higher education, even 220 years after Wesley's death.

We'll start our look at Wesley's theology[6] at the same point where Richard Hughes started his look at Reformed theology—the sovereignty of God. Wesley centers God's sovereignty as the act of creation. Designing all that exists from absolute nothing is an act of God's ultimate power. He sees God having a deep sense of order that we cannot begin to understand. The result, from our perspective, is one of awe and wonder. We know of God's creative power because He has revealed it to us in scripture. We also confirm that in what we see around us. The Creation itself tells us of God's power.

Yet Wesley is also looking forward to the fulfillment of that Creation. It is still occurring in our midst and centers on the faithfulness of the Image of God. Theodore Runyon summarizes:

> The image of God is hardly a new motif; it is familiar not only from the Genesis account of creation but from New Testament accounts of restoration and renewal. (1998, p. 8)

In contrast to the Deists of his day, who saw God as distant and uninvolved, Wesley saw God as working toward the redemption of what was lost in the Fall: the image of God that He implanted in us at the Creation. This image is the measure of our moral nature. This doesn't detract from the Fall. But the Fall initiates God's reach to us through the incarnation and sacrifice of Jesus and the ongoing work of the Holy Spirit.

In his book, *Responsible Grace*, Randy Maddox argues that the consistent theme, or *"orienting concern,"* throughout Wesley's life is that God extends his grace to us (while we are yet sinners) and that we have an individual responsibility to respond to that offer by either accepting or rejecting it. If we accept the offer of relationship, we engage in an ongoing process of growing in that grace. Maddox summarizes the process of responsible grace as follows:

---

6. Randy Maddox (1994) explains that Wesley was more of a practical theologian than a systematic theologian. In other words, he wasn't developing overall systems of thought as much as impacting the lives of Christians.

Wesley understood Prevenient Grace[7] to be God's initial move toward restored relationship with fallen humanity. As a first dimension, this involved God's merciful removal of any inherited guilt, by virtue of Christ. A second dimension of God's initial move to restored Presence is a partial healing of our debilitated human faculties, sufficient for us to sense and respond to God. The final dimension is God's specific overtures to individuals, inviting closer relationship. If these overtures are welcomed, a grace-empowered relationship of co-operative and progressive transformation sets forth. Since God's grace is universal, so is the possibility of such relationship. Since God's grace is resistible, no individual's participation is inevitable. (p. 90)

Runyon says that Wesley thought of God's offering of grace and our response to it as a form of "spiritual respiration" and quotes one of Wesley's sermons:

God's breathing into the soul, and the soul's breathing back what it first receives from God; a continual *action* of God upon the soul, the *re-action* of the soul upon God; an unceasing presence of God, the loving, pardoning God, manifested to the heart, and perceived by faith; and an unceasing return of love, praise, and prayer, offering up all the thoughts of our hearts, all the words of our tongues, all the works of our hands, all our body, soul, and spirit, to be an holy sacrifice, acceptable unto God in Christ Jesus. (Quoted in Runyon, 1998, p. 18; italics Wesley's)

Maddox traces Wesley's appropriation of theological concepts from Eastern Christianity. Drawing upon the writings of early church fathers influenced by Greek writers, Wesley articulated a very different understanding of major theological concepts than his Western counterparts:

[T]he dominant streams of Western Christianity eventually affirmed two major effects of the Fall upon subsequent humanity: (1) we inherit the guilt of the Original Sin; and (2) as one sign of God's judgment, our human faculties are depraved to the point that we are free to do little more than sin. Eastern Christianity has vigorously denied both of these effects. They contend that the true significance of the Fall was our loss of the Spirit's immediate Presence, resulting in the introduction of mortality into human life. This mortality weakened our human faculties and effaced our

---

7. Prevenient Grace is the proactive reach of God toward us even before we are aware of it.

moral Likeness of God. Thus, *the Fall did render us prone to sin, but not incapable of co-operating with God's offer of healing.* (1994, p. 74, emphasis mine)

How does this co-operation occur? Wesley maintained that God's outreach to humanity occurred through the work of the Holy Spirit in human lives. This work begins before the individual is even aware of God and continues through salvation and further growth in discipleship to the ultimate goal of holy living. Maddox quotes a key passage from one of Wesley's letters that describes this role:

I believe the infinite and eternal Spirit of God, equal with the Father and the Son, to be not only perfectly holy . . . but the immediate cause of all holiness in us; *enlightening our understandings, rectifying our wills and affections,* renewing our natures, uniting our persons to Christ, assuring us of the adoption of sons, leading us in our actions, purifying and sanctifying our souls and bodies to a full and eternal enjoyment of God. (p. 123, emphasis mine)

Wesley argued that the Holy Spirit, through God's work of prevenient grace, enlivens our "spiritual senses."[8] Jason Vickers describes Wesley's focus:

In his appeal to the Spirit's work in restoring the spiritual senses, Wesley recognized both the devastating effects of sin and the sheer gratuity of salvation. In his retrieval of the doctrine of the inner witness, he offered a solution to a long-standing and widespread problem within Protestantism that was spiritually disabling for many people. (Vickers, 2010, p. 205)

The sovereign God helps us see the moral implications of our actions even while we're still far off. The work of the Spirit enlightens understandings in a number of ways. It's what happens when that worship song "rings true" or when the reading from Dostoyevsky suddenly sounds like Gospel. It's what happens when a conversation with friends becomes a moment of clarity regarding your life's calling (or this month's version of it).

One of the primary ways the Holy Spirit touches us is through what Wesley called the "means of grace." These would include the sacraments (communion and baptism) but also more "ordinary" activities like prayer and Bible reading. As Howard Snyder observes, Wesley sees these activities

8. Southern Methodist theologian William Abraham provides an excellent summary of how Wesley thought of Spiritual Senses (Abraham, 2010).

as truly "means, not ends" (Snyder, 1980). They don't provide grace in and of themselves, but become the avenue through which grace can be received.

This is what occurred in Wesley's own life at the moment of his famous "Aldersgate Street" experience. One Wednesday night when he was thirty-five, he was meeting with friends for a study of Martin Luther's Preface to Romans. Suddenly he was overwhelmed by the sense of the Spirit's assurance that he was truly forgiven. Not that he wasn't already a Christian, but he became freshly aware of the Spirit's presence (Vickers, 2010, p. 205).

Wesley may not have been striving after God's assurance that night. He may have just been going along with his regular meeting group. But, as he points out in a later sermon on Means of Grace, participating in scriptural study can be effective "also for those who are yet in darkness, seeking him whom they know not" (Wesley, 1746).

Consistent in all these views of Wesley, then, is a sense that God is reaching to us through His Spirit, seeking to restore us to our intended image and motivations as we act in grateful obedience to the outreach made to us. The door is flung open and we are invited in. We have but to respond.

Before moving to how we respond, I want to follow the pattern Richard Hughes set to suggest some educational implications of what we've seen in Wesley so far. First, Wesley suggests that the Spirit can enlighten our human frailties. Our task is to be responsive to the light we're shown, whether that happens in chapel or in French class.

Second, God is continually creating; new information, challenging reading, difficulty conversations are the avenues through which this can happen. That's the lesson of Peter's vision in the opening chapter. God is still in sovereign control and we need not feel like he must be protected from challenging subjects or situations.

Third, we must be attentive to the means of grace—not simply the expected "religious" ones like chapel or accountability groups, but to recognize the importance of the daily patterns of our lives. Even issues like going to sociology class or doing accounting homework can operate like ordinary sacraments.

Howard Snyder suggested that there is a synthesis between Wesley's approach to theology and his practice. There are also some important educational implications that come from those. I'll review Wesley's method and then look at how it was put into practice.

The "Wesleyan Quadrilateral" of scripture, tradition, reason, and experience isn't really a four-sided image. Nearly all Wesley scholars see scripture as primary for Wesley. But that scripture was seen in concert with the traditions of the church and the experiences of the individual. Then, through the application of Spirit-enlightened reason, one made sense of what was read in order to engage in obedient practice. Snyder has recently suggested we need a "pentalateral," with Creation joining the other three to form a quadrilateral surrounding the central Scripture (2009).

Two thoughts about Wesley's view of scripture. First, while primary, it was to be read in concert with other sources. Scott Jones observes that Wesley chastised his preachers who only read the Bible (Snyder, 2011). Wesley believed we needed to be aware of the Book of Nature[9] as well.

Second, we need to guard against reading scripture only through the lens of our own experience. Not only should we read for the major overarching themes of scripture and avoid proof-texting with isolated passages (which Wesley disliked) but we needed to hear how others were reading those themes. Here's advice from two Wesleyan biblical scholars just out of emerging adulthood:

> We benefit not only from *listening* to other interpretations in contexts different than our own. We benefit even more from *inhabiting* those contexts . . . Learning to read from the perspective of others takes a good deal of imagination. It may require that we set aside some of our assumptions about the "plain meaning" of the biblical text, if only for a few moments. When we try to see how others might read a text, it opens up new avenues for understanding a passage. And it gives us more compassion for others in general. (Lyons-Pardue & Sturdevant, 2011, pp. 154–55; italics in original)

Wesley's view of tradition is also helpful for the twenty-first century. He centered his vision of the church within a narrow period of history— beginning with the establishment of the original Christian movement up to Constantine's decision to make Christianity the faith of the empire. Wesley held that that earlier vision could teach us much about the Christian life.

This is significant. One of the sociological challenges to the Christian faith occurs when it becomes too blended with the power and apparatus of the civil society. Vibrant faith, to Wesley, means to take the scriptural record seriously. As Maddox observes, we build on the faith traditions of those who've gone before but we're able to learn from missteps as well as from models of devotion. That means that tradition is continually unfolding.

---

9. That's how Wesley referred to our understanding of the natural world around us.

As we've already seen, experience is important to Wesley in a very personal way. The significance of the Spirit's affirmation that he was a child of God cannot be overstressed. But experience for Wesley also means that we're paying attention to what goes on around us. We see how we interact with others. We are aware of how we're changing. The experiences we have are raw materials we're using to construct faith.

Wesley's approach to reason is not the same as those who have an exaggerated view of the power of logical thought. He saw reason as a means of working out the relationships between the other components of his system. It means to think carefully about what one reads or hears and to reflect on how it comports with scripture and tradition.

So then, we are formed as Christians through understanding the broad strokes of scripture, through reflection on our experiences, through lovingly sorting through past traditions, and through using our brains as enlivened by the Spirit's leading. As we will see in chapter 8, this means that the total of the Christian university experience is part of the whole of faith development. Sure, it's easier to see that in chapel or in Old Testament class. But it's also operating when you're at Denny's at 2:00 in the morning, when you're doing calculus homework, or playing Ultimate Frisbee with friends.

As you can see, Wesley's method was thoughtful, yet messy. There would appear to be a lot of space in the midst of the interplay between the factors.[10] One comes up with tentative conclusions and then must hold them loosely while testing them. As we will see, we need each other to stay grounded in the midst of exploration.

There is a danger of an over-individualized view of faith. Think of our earlier look at Jeff Bethke's video. Perhaps emerging adults in our Selective Adherent camp would find comfort in a smorgasbord approach to meaning-making, but Wesley takes us a different direction.

To address an over-individualized faith, Wesley required new converts to join classes. Howard Snyder suggests:

> [O]nce a structure and practice of community were instituted, the church began to function biblically as a church, as body of Christ . . . [T]heir primary purpose was discipline. (Snyder, 1980)

10. My university has a clock tower with the four elements of the quadrilateral on each face. In one of my classes, I walk the students around the outside and we talk about what each means. Then we step in the middle to show where the real work takes place.

Oftentimes, such discipline could be pretty intrusive, with leaders asking for accountability regarding one's temptations and failings. But people being together in groups made a difference.

There were also larger groups called Bands and even larger ones called Societies. The important point is that the members shared their lives together. Furthermore, they tested their tentative understandings with one another. The testing is not about seeking orthodoxy or keeping people on the "straight and narrow." Rebekah Miles puts it well: "Reason alone can accomplish very little; reason in good company can do many things"(Miles, 1997). She continues:

> [R]eason's work is not a self-enclosed, individual task. Reason's extent depends on the abundant resources of the environment, including discourse with other people and traditions. Reason always works in conversation. Thus, Christian "conference" is necessary to theological reasoning. This Wesleyan point is especially important in the current debates around postmodernity . . . At the same time, conference allows us greater confidence in those claims that we do arrive at together. This Wesleyan model of reason as a tool that can reflect on experience is less grand than some modern claims about reason, but it is also more substantial than some postmodern suspicion of reason. (1997, p. 103)

To be dependent upon others in response to grace is to recognize that we are co-learners together. We are working to bring each other into the establishment of moral living, sound thinking, and right will. This is true in any group we are with and not just those like us. This is the lesson Peter learned when meeting Cornelius.

Implications

What does this mean for you as a Christian university student? It means that all of the people around you are part of God's "method" of helping you grow. Your professors may challenge you with new ideas that make you question traditional understandings. But they don't want you to stop with questions. They want to be part of your growing and development into what God intends for you to be. But there's more: you are part of their growing and shaping into what God intends for them to be. They must reflect on what they've learned in the midst of the class you took and use that to become better disciples.

It means that the time you spend with mentors—coaches and advisors—aren't simply exercises in people telling you the rules. They're the ways you learn how to perform in your own unique way. A coach won't simply teach you how to handle a tennis volley but wants you to handle that volley in a way that works within your overall style. You still have to get the ball over the net, but it's about your development.

It means that the time you spend with friends is a place of accountability and mutuality. Not just when you're in formal discipleship groups or mission outings, but in classes and over lunch and at ball games.

In other words, all of the Christian university experience is caught up in working through what God has created you to be. Everything is part of the "stuff" from which you exercise your spiritual senses to move forward in your journey.

I can't overestimate this reality. What keeps you from fear and panic about the uncertainty of emerging adulthood is that you aren't alone. The Holy Spirit of God is active in our midst. Often that Spirit does what he does through those around us. What makes the Christian university special is that we have the audacity to embrace this miraculous vision.

Earlier in this chapter, I introduced you to Tom Oord's view of revisionary postmodernism. Consider how his view aligns with what the task of constructing the Kingdom of God:

> We live in a new world. Postmodernism reminds us of that. Revisionary postmodernism promotes the task of constructing a new worldview to account for truths in the widest range of experience. It places God and creation front and center. (Oord, 2010)

We started this review of Wesley's theology with his recognition that the Creator God *in the beginning* is creating now and will continue to do so in preparation for the Coming Kingdom. This ongoing Creation reinforces an idea we saw earlier: our stories, while important, are part of a Larger Story God is writing. When we engage others in Christian dialogue, while listening for the leading of the Spirit, we are practicing the principles of that Kingdom that Jesus said was at hand (Mark 1:15). Howard Snyder concludes:

> What does all this mean of the life and experience of the church today? Primarily that we must determine our understanding of the Kingdom of God and of the church's agency in the Kingdom of God on the basis of the biblical revelation. The body of Christ is to

be an eschatological and messianic[11] community of the Kingdom
in a more fundamentally important sense that Wesley understood.
(Snyder, 1980, p. 160)

The task of the Christian university is no more and no less than this.
It's true that we're in the middle of learning and teaching and living. But
that's just what we're doing. It may be another form of the means of grace,
but it's really the place where we experience the current and coming Kingdom of God. What an exciting prospect! We'll explore the specifics of how
we live that out over the next several chapters.

---

11. Eschatological means we're concerned with the fulfillment of God's vision. Messianic means we're concerned with bringing others to Christ in their response to God's
grace.

6

People Like Me

The week before classes began, you likely participated in what colleges refer to as "orientation." It's a compressed time (a few days to a week) that confronts you with information about the school you chose: where things are, what the policy details are that you didn't really pay attention to during recruiting ("we have chapel?"), faculty members' academic expectations, and time for bonding—lots of bonding. In the midst of that, you're sleeping in a strange place while dealing with being away from your home, parents, and friends, all the while never letting on that you might be a tad bit homesick.

It would be more accurate to call this week "disorientation" because you have all this new information to absorb. Some folks want you to focus on building relationships (the "tin men") while others want you to understand the expectations of academic life (the "scarecrows"). Plus, you are surrounded by strangers. Their experiences are far different from yours, you don't really understand each other, and yet somehow the university expects you to form life-long friendships! It's a lot to process.

The title of this chapter has two meanings. The tension between those two meanings is key to building the kind of community that lies at the heart of Christian higher education.

The first meaning is borrowed from an old Saturday Night Live skit. Al Franken, now a U.S. Senator from Minnesota, occasionally appeared as a character named Stuart Smalley. In a skit known as "Daily Affirmation," Stuart performed a monologue on a number of life issues but always ended by looking deeply in the mirror and saying to himself, *"I'm good enough, I'm smart enough, and doggone it, people like me."* Stuart wanted to be known as himself, not as some caricature of himself. He wanted to be affirmed in his identity. The fact that he ended each skit only talking to himself illustrates how much of a challenge he found affirmation to be.

As you start in a new environment, especially one involving the major life transition discussed in this book, you want to be who you really are. You want that identity to be understood and appreciated by others. In other words, people "like" me.

Being with others gets at the second meaning of the title. We find ourselves drawn to those who share our understandings, experiences, hopes, and dreams. It's captured in the adage, "*Birds of a feather flock together.*" Not only do we want to be affirmed in who we are, we want to simultaneously fit in. Thus, we desire to be around "people like" me.

In my experience, finding your place may be harder in a Christian university environment than it would be at the big state school. That's somewhat paradoxical in that we saw earlier that many people choose a Christian university so that they'll belong. They're searching for a community of like-minded believers (or at least folks who will support the community).

Much of my time in Christian higher education has been in schools connected to a particular denomination. While the majority of students didn't come from that denomination, they all came expecting (or accepting) certain "Christian" givens.

Part of the transition from the home church to the university is you discover that people don't necessarily see things just as you do. They may see the Bible as inerrant (or not) or support women in ministry (or not). They may believe different things about proper means of baptism, the nature of the second coming, or the meaning of social justice. Their families may have voted for Democrats (or Republicans)!

These discoveries of difference are not limited to folks from other church backgrounds. It's even more disorienting for someone who grew up in the sponsoring denomination to discover that other students who grew up in the same denomination are so different. Because many students grow up in homogeneous churches, they come to assume "this is what it means to be _____ (fill in denomination here)."

Students attending the large state university didn't expect to find similarity. They'll find their belonging by simply being one of the Christian students. Intervarsity Fellowship is built around that kind of bonding.

To find out in your state school that the guy in the next room doesn't believe in Jesus is not shocking. Being at a Christian school and discovering that the guy next door favors women in ministry may be a big deal.

Thinking about Community

This chapter will examine how we navigate the tensions between identity, difference, and belonging. As we will see, it can be tempting to jump over those tensions in favor of "everyone just getting along" or "agreeing to disagree." We need to move toward true community, which provides the opportunity for the university to be an outpost of the Kingdom of God. This task of working through differences is at the center of what it means to participate in the larger world. What is learned in the laboratory of the Christian university will be played out thousands of times in the world beyond it.

Christian schools should engage this process precisely because society in general is so bad at it. The broader society seems to oscillate between demands for individual recognition and group conformity. When Christians try to explore the process of holding the two in tension, we wind up taking unhelpful shortcuts.

It's easy to see these patterns in the movies. It's a fairly standard setup. Start with a group of misfits and find a plot device where they must overcome their differences. Even the misfits follow fairly predictable patterns.

One is highly intelligent but suffers from a lack of social graces. Another is muscular but not very smart. A third is something of a con artist, able to talk his way through any impossible situation. A fourth is a pretty, popular girl from a wealthy home that everyone knows is stuck up. A fifth will not interact with others and seems completely inwardly focused. A sixth is the "girl-next-door" who is always taken for granted and doesn't realize her true beauty. A seventh would be classified as a slacker, a stoner, or a drunkard (and maybe all three).

I'm sure you can come up with any number of films or television shows that build on this device. Caper movies, situation comedies, adventure/fantasy films, and teen-coming-of-age comedies all use it. I'm pretty sure I can make this theme work for recent popular films like *The Hunger Games* (2012) or *Twilight* (2008).

However, it was *The Mighty Ducks* (Herek, 1992) that first drew my attention to how society turns difference into community with such seeming simplicity. I liked the movie a lot. It had heart, showed redemption of past mistakes, showed good overcoming arrogance, and celebrated interdependence. The sociological message, though, seemed to be that all those quirky differences (they had a girl playing hockey!) were really the glue that made them all work. They acknowledged what each brought to the ice, learned to count on it, and grew as people through the hardship of competition.

In real life, tough competition, new uniforms, and "believing in ourselves" is not enough to build community. Community takes hard work and requires us to deal with issues that we'd rather not deal with. As we will see, things get messy before they get better. Life isn't like the movies that reach happy closure in one hundred minutes.

So let's go back to orientation and explore how community really works. Imagine that two eager, freshman students, Becky and Sarah, have been assigned as roommates. Because they are members of this tech-friendly generation, they've been in regular contact via Facebook and Twitter since the spring. They've even created a Pinterest page to work out the room decor.

But there are other issues the girls haven't begun to consider. Becky is an only child who enjoys a large bedroom, a queen-sized bed, her own computer, stereo, and television, and has her own bathroom. Her family lives in a nice suburb in a major metropolitan area. She and her parents think nothing of heading downtown to the art museum and dinner in a fancy restaurant. They've been to Europe twice as a family and Becky did a two-week mission trip with the youth group from her church (affiliated with the denomination that sponsors the university).

Sarah is one of four daughters, has always had a twin bed, shared a room with one of her sisters, and had to carefully schedule her morning preparation time as she shared a single bathroom with the entire family. Sarah's family lives in a small town thirty minutes from the county seat, which houses the only movie theatre within ninety minutes of her house. Vacations consist of twice-annual trips to see grandparents two hours away. She and her family attend a non-denominational church of about one hundred people. Sarah is the first person on either side of her family to attend college.

Becky and Sarah's Orientation runs on a high degree of energy with all the excitement of newness. The room gets decorated as planned and has already drawn praise from the other residents in the hall. The parents have gone home, classes have begun, and the girls start falling into a routine.

Becky and Sarah will need to develop a robust understanding of the processes of building community if they are to affirm their individual identity while learning to navigate their differences. Let's use their situation to unpack some of the social science of community building.

The late psychologist M. Scott Peck, in addition to writing his famous personal development books (*The Road Less Traveled* [1978] being the best known), devoted much of his career to community building. Over many years, he led hundreds of individuals through workshops designed to deepen their sense of community. He discovered that our deep cultural commitments to individualism have blinded us to the dynamics of the communities that surround us, creating "*a hole in our minds.*"

> The hole in our minds under discussion relates primarily to the poverty of our consciousness of organizations and systems . . .The problem is not so much one of physical as of mental distance. Actually, the organization is every bit as close as our neighbor, so close that it may be hard to see the threads binding us as we talk across our desks or backyard fences. Being invisible, however, the web of such threads—the organization—is abstract and tends to seem, therefore, far more distant that it really is. (Peck, 1993, p. 30)

Because we lack broader understandings of our connectedness to others and therefore do not engage in the work of building community, we are tempted to live an isolated existence, attempting to be an island unto ourselves.

In the college setting, the result of the lack of awareness that Peck describes is that students, faculty, and administrators mistake their connections as emotional closeness. In every college in which I've worked, students have remarked that their faculty know them by name.

Surprisingly, a focus on emotionality, warmth, and belonging can actually inhibit the development of the community. In a close setting, the primary focus of all members of the group is to smooth over differences by keeping them inside, avoiding conflict, and staying close to those others who already agree. The primary motivation is to maintain politeness.

Scott Peck refers to this initial stage of community formation as *Pseudocommunity*. In order to remain conflict-avoidant, he says, participants in a pseudocommunity work hard at ignoring individual differences, he writes:

> In pseudocommunity it is as if every individual member is operating according to the same book of etiquette. The rules of this book are: Don't do or say anything that might offend someone else; if someone does or says something that offends, annoys, or irritates you, act as if nothing has happened and pretend you are not bothered in the least; and if some form of disagreement

should show signs of appearing, change the subject as quickly as possible—rules that any good hostess knows. It is easy to see how these rules make for a smoothly functioning group. But they also crush individuality, intimacy, honesty, and the longer it lasts the duller it gets. (pp. 88–89)

What does pseudocommunity mean for Becky and Sarah? At some point fairly early on, as the novelty wears a bit, they will begin to confront the issues imbedded in their preferences, needs, or personal styles. Serious negotiations must take place: will the room be clean or "lived in," is there shared space or individual space, are clothes interchangeable or personal property, what kind of music will be played and at what hours, do studies or social activities come first?

Attempts to simply commit to each other "in Christian love" will quickly give way to periodic arguments, hurt feelings, episodes of silence, and heated phone calls home. Naïve hopes that "it will all work out," as it does in the movies, will lead to disappointment and discouragement. Such disappointment isn't given voice however. That would violate the norms of pseudocommunity. So they will likely talk to each other a little less, make sure they are in the presence of a group of others, and make the best of things.

Becky is sure that Sarah is a hick. Sarah is sure that Becky is a pampered brat. Internally, they may begin planning for new roommates next semester or at least next year. What they won't do is talk about their differences. Sure, they'll talk about trivial things like who was up too late or who is too noisy, but they won't *really* talk. All energy is committed to maintaining peace above everything else.

Pseudocommunity isn't really about the interpersonal relationships between roommates. It's part of a larger configuration of relationships in families, churches, workplaces, and even Christian universities. Becky and Sarah allow us to explore the process of community development. Keep in mind that we are taking what we learn from them and expanding to include a much larger web of connections.

In the college setting, we can be tempted to place the same value on minimizing conflict. While we may be aware of individual differences, we don't explore those too deeply because to take them seriously complicates our common task. *Pseudocommunities celebrate the idea of community without actually building one.* They speak in generalities and not specifics, according to Peck. If we focused on specifics we'd have to work through differing definitions and interpretations. But if we celebrate the importance of individuals without getting to know them deeply, we can simply feel good about the vague idea of community.

At some point during the fall semester, the discussions between Becky and Sarah begin to violate the norms of pseudocommunity. This will probably follow some predictable cycle of an academic semester. Around the end of October, all the novelty has worn off but there is a lot of time left before Christmas break. Whatever the trigger event is, it becomes the "one more thing" that can't be tolerated any longer. Words are spoken that cause pain. RAs are brought in to mediate. Housing directors may consider whether finding new roommates for spring would be a good idea.

Peck calls this stage "chaos;" a critical testing point for the development of community. The pair of roommates must face and overcome chaos and conflict if community is to form. If the chaos is denied, they will live "happily" as acquaintances for a while but will never develop a deep relationship. Peck observes that the individual differences themselves become the very sources of conflict:

> In the stage of chaos, individual differences are, unlike those in pseudocommunity, right out in the open. Only now, instead of trying to hide or ignore them, the group is attempting to obliterate them. Underlying the attempts to heal and convert is not so much the motive of love as the motive to make everyone *normal*—and the motive to win, as the members fight over whose norm might prevail. (1987, p. 91, emphasis in original)

The arguments between the roommates will not be about how to resolve the real issues described earlier (where to put the stereo, sharing clothes, study hours) but about which set of personal experiences should have the most validity in the current situation. Becky will be challenged to learn to share and stop acting like a spoiled kid. Sarah will be challenged to stop looking at the world from her small town perspective. Each roommate will attempt to show the superiority of her past.

To be responsible for individual differences and incorporate them truthfully into the fabric of the community is to invite chaos and conflict. It is worth noting that this is a specific outgrowth of postmodernism. One of the critiques frequently offered of postmodernism is that recognition of individual-level values makes it impossible to determine whose views are "*right*." Concern is expressed that there are no longer objective standards for determining which view takes precedence over another. In the modern view (the view shaped by the Enlightenment), these objective assumptions are key to a common understanding of the scientific, empirical world. In the postmodern view, such assumptions must be mediated through individual interpretations.

While he doesn't put his argument in postmodern terms, I think Peck would completely agree that he is advocating a postmodern approach, not as an end in itself but as the means to community. The presence of diverse stories requires the hard work that shapes true community. If we are able to rely on power structures to define how we are supposed to fit in, then we simply return to the quiet conformity of pseudocommunity. To take individual differences seriously requires us to willingly enter into chaos in order for us to truly become a community.

Becky and Sarah are going to have some unpleasant days of chaos. The business of college life may allow them to avoid each other, but eventually they'll go back to the room and have to deal with it. When they start really hearing each other, they discover new difficulties but the rewards on the other side give hope.

This is Peck's third stage: "emptiness." Parker Palmer, the sociologist and educator we met earlier, has a rule for how emptiness works: "No fixing, no saving, no setting each other straight" (Palmer, 2004). To follow this rule means abandoning control over another. It means allowing others to truly be who they are as a step toward coming together. It is nothing less than what Jesus calls "losing your life to save it" (Mark 8:35).

This is a very difficult step. To engage in emptiness requires us to stop caring about our personal stake in a particular outcome. It means that we search for calm in the midst of the chaos.

When I lived in Kansas, watching tornados and other severe storms was a normal activity. During the storm, it was important to stay away from windows and watch for the development of hailstones, tornados, or wind damage. But after the storm, there would be a moment of calm when the wind stopped and the air cooled. I see the move from chaos to emptiness as that kind of sensation.

Daniel Goleman and his colleagues analyzed the importance of emotional intelligence in organizational life (Goleman, Boyatzis, & McKee, 2002). People with high degrees of emotional intelligence know how to align their own emotions, activities, and motivations with the emotions of the others around them. They are aware of what others are feeling and how those emotions can impact the group as a whole.

Emptiness becomes easier to achieve as individuals and groups grow in the key characteristics of emotional intelligence: self-awareness, self-management, social awareness, and relationship management. A Christian university must put a high priority on the development of these four skills if it is to assist its students and faculty to navigate from chaos to community.

Becky must really hear Sarah from deep in her being without trying to make Sarah into what she wishes she could be. Sarah must give Becky the same space. Not as a negotiation strategy or problem solving exercise, but as a matter of Christian love.

Let me again remind you that what Becky and Sarah are going through is being repeated in relationships all over campus. These may be relationships between new students and continuing students, between classmates and faculty members, between students and parents, or between players and coaches. But all must deal with emptiness if community is the goal.

Emptiness, then, is not a one-time achievement but is more of an attitude over the long-haul. The result of this long-term commitment to emotional intelligence and validating the other is that the emptiness that accompanies loss of control gives way to something more significant. Peck describes this significant change in the life of the group:

> I have spoken of the stage of emptiness largely as if it were something that occurs solely within the minds and souls of the individuals who compose a group. But community is always something more than the sum total of the individuals present. Pseudocommunity, chaos, and emptiness are not so much individual stages as group stages. The transformation of a group from a collection of individuals into genuine community requires little deaths in many of those individuals. But it is also a process of group death, group dying . . .
>
> Whether sudden or gradual, however, all the groups in my experience have eventually succeeded in completing, accomplishing this death. They have all made it through emptiness, through the time of sacrifice, into community. This is an extraordinary testament to the human spirit. What it means is that given the right circumstances and knowledge of the rules, on a certain but very real level we human beings are able to die for each other.[1] (pp. 102–3)

As Peck describes it, the emerging community may not be clearly conscious of what is happening in their midst. He frequently describes this as involving moments of group silence where listening to the others in the

---

1. This has deep theological parallels. See 1 John 3:16.

group seems to become more important than preparing the next remark. In the times I have been most aware of this process, it seems that something larger than the individuals involved is driving the conversation and deepening the understanding. The individuals seem to be reacting to that larger understanding and not directly to each other. Our ability to attend to the Holy Spirit is critically important to life in the Christian university. This is the key to becoming a community.

It is far easier to describe this process than to accomplish it in real life. Perhaps another metaphor will illustrate the "letting go" involved in emptiness. One of my favorite passages in the late Douglas Adams' *The Hitchhiker's Guide to the Galaxy* trilogy (Adams, 1981) is when the Guide explains how to fly (sorry, it's too much to try and explain it here, read the book or find the YouTube videos): "*The knack [of flying]*," says the Guide, "*lies in learning how to throw yourself at the ground and miss.*" If chaos is throwing yourself at the ground, emptiness abandons chaos. As Palmer says, you stop trying to fix things. It's just as effortless as flying.

Community is not something to be readily achieved but something that we constantly strive for. It is an ongoing process and not a point of destination. To maintain it over time requires deep relationships that affirm individual identity while seeing the group as a source of meaning. The process of community has the potential to extend beyond itself, even though it is guaranteed to move through Peck's stages again and again as it grows closer to some ideal. Peck describes the ongoing nature of community development:

> If a community—or part of it—does decide to maintain itself, it will have many new tasks. Community maintenance requires that multiple major decisions be made or remade over extensive periods of time. The community will frequently fall back into chaos or even pseudocommunity in the process. Over and again it will need to do the agonizing work of reemptying itself. Many groups fail here. (1993, pp. 104–5)

Scott Peck's work on community formation demonstrates that it is hard work indeed. As we have seen, much of higher education is designed to promote individual achievement and personal performance. Too often, others are considered primarily as obstacles to avoid or tools to be used in achieving our personal goals. But the possibilities inherent in a commitment to community life move us beyond the polite safety of individual achievement. They move us first into places where we would rather not be, because they are terribly uncomfortable. As we move into those uncomfortable spaces, we find that we are forced to see that the world we have imagined for our own benefit is not the real world. We begin to examine the worlds that others have created. If we stay with that difficult task and maintain a deep sense of trust, we begin to find that there is a larger world we hadn't considered. In that new, larger world, community can make room for all of the individual worlds.

Community as God's Gift

This, of course, is what the Apostle Paul is getting at when using body imagery to describe the Christian community:

> For through the grace given to me I say to everyone among you not to think more highly of himself than he ought to think; but to think so as to have sound judgment, as God has allotted to each a measure of faith. For just as we have many members in one body and all the members do not have the same function, so we, who are many, are one body in Christ, and individually members one of another. Since we have gifts that differ according to the grace given to us, each of us is to exercise them accordingly: if prophecy, according to the proportion of his faith; if service, in his serving; or he who teaches, in his teaching; or he who exhorts, in his exhortation; he who gives, with liberality; he who leads, with diligence; he who shows mercy, with cheerfulness. (Romans 12:3–8)

Paul reminds us that the expression of our uniqueness is possible in direct relationship to our faith. To believe that we were created for a purpose requires that we play our individual roles to the fullest extent possible.

We can't anticipate the ways in which Becky will help Sarah grow into the person God prepares her to be. We can't know how Sarah will support Becky in times of crisis. But each of them is affirming a unique, God-given identity. The same is true for all the other students they go to school with.

What Paul says doesn't stop with an image of individual performance. In his first letter to Corinth, he takes the body imagery even more seriously. Each person still represents a part of the Body of Christ but the lesson here is about our interdependence more than our unique role:

> For the body is not one member, but many. If the foot says, "Because I am not a hand, I am not a part of the body," it is not for this reason any the less a part of the body. And if the ear says,

> "Because I am not an eye, I am not a part of the body," it is not for this reason any the less a part of the body. If the whole body were an eye, where would the hearing be? If the whole were hearing, where would the sense of smell be? But now God has placed the members, each one of them, in the body, just as He desired. If they were all one member, where would the body be? But now there are many members, but one body. And the eye cannot say to the hand, "I have no need of you"; or again the head to the feet, "I have no need of you." On the contrary, it is much truer that the members of the body which seem to be weaker are necessary; and those members of the body which we deem less honorable, on these we bestow more abundant honor, and our less presentable members become much more presentable, whereas our more presentable members have no need of it. But God has so composed the body, giving more abundant honor to that member which lacked, so that there may be no division in the body, but that the members may have the same care for one another. And if one member suffers, all the members suffer with it; if one member is honored, all the members rejoice with it. Now you are Christ's body, and individually members of it. (1 Corinthians 12: 14–27)

Paul's image is a powerful one indeed. It suggests that each of us must recognize our unique contribution to the larger community and then empty ourselves of the need to be in charge. For one of us to proclaim that his needs trump all others is no different than the eye complaining that it is not given sufficient control over the body. For one of us to hold back, because we think no one would want to hear from us, is to fail to understand Paul's comments about the essential value of the supposedly weaker member.

Becky and Sarah are stronger together than either of them are individually. They belong to others. And that belonging allows a vibrant life uninhibited by the fears and limitations of being eighteen.

If we are to live in authentic community, we must move beyond Peck's simple stages of community building. We recognize that our unique understanding and our individual definition of the situation must be shared with one another if we are truly to be the Body of Christ.

Dietrich Bonhoeffer wrote *Life Together* as a reflection on his experiences at the Finkenwalde seminary. It is a careful examination of the theological connotations of the concept of community. Central to Bonhoeffer's argument is the belief that true community is something that we are given by God:

> It is easily forgotten that the fellowship of Christian brethren is a gift of grace, a gift of the Kingdom of God that any day may be taken from us, that the time that still separates us from utter loneliness may be brief indeed. Therefore, let him who until now has had the privilege of living a common Christian life with other Christians praise God's grace from the bottom of his heart. Let him thank God on his knees and declare: It Is grace, nothing but grace, that we are allowed to live in community with Christian brethren. (Bonhoeffer, 1954, p. 20)

Bonhoeffer's view of community provides a helpful corrective to Scott Peck's work. Peck seems to suggest that community can be formed if only we learn how to empty ourselves of preconceptions, prejudices, and power. If only we try really, really hard and willingly enter into chaos then we can find ourselves in community. It seems that he is suggesting that we work hard in preparation to abandon barriers and then *"get out of the way"* as community emerges.

Bonhoeffer reminds us that *we can't make community happen.* In fact, our attempts to create versions of community may actually inhibit the formation of true Christian community.

> Every human wish dream that is injected into the Christian community is a hindrance to genuine community and must be banished if genuine community is to survive. He who lives his dream of a community more than the Christian community itself becomes a destroyer of the latter, even though his personal intentions may be ever so honest and earnest and sacrificial. (p. 27)

So while Peck's vision of community is essentially social psychological (relating to patterns of interaction among group members), Bonhoeffer's vision of community is fundamentally theological (placing the community in its proper relationship with God). This is not to suggest that these are incompatible visions, but they begin in different places. The psychological approach reminds us of the challenges present in the pursuit of community. The theological orientation helps us understand why it is that community is a grace.

Becky and Sarah are, in a real way, gifts to each other. Seen in this light, their occasional challenges and adjustments aren't obstacles, but opportunities.

Bonhoeffer recognizes that the essence of true community lies not in our personal preferences or our learning styles or our strengths, but in our common relationship to Jesus Christ. He suggests that our need for salvation moves us from seeing self as the solution to our problems to seeing Jesus as the solution. We become focused on others because we recognize that our own weakness leaves us in need of salvation from another place.

Furthermore, Bonhoeffer argues that the only way we can really relate to others is because of the love of Christ born in us. If we rely only on our own strength, our selves get in the way of truly relating to others:

> Without Christ we should not know God, we could not call upon Him, nor come to Him. But without Christ we also would not know our brother, nor could we come to him. The way is blocked by our own ego. Christ opened up the way to God and to our brother. Now Christians can live with one another in peace; they can love and serve one another; they can become one. (pp. 23–24)

It is because we accept the love of Christ that we can love one another. His sacrifice removes the guilt and shame that inhibit our relationship to others. He does the same for their relationships with us. Christ's sacrifice provides us with a model and a means to build relationship (see Philippians 2:6–8).

Finally, Bonhoeffer suggests that Christ's incarnation opens the possibility for us to be bound together. Because Christ identified with us when he became flesh, his nature is connected to our nature. Conversely, our nature is tied up in His. This is not true only for us individually; it is also true for us collectively:

> We belong to him because we are in him. That is why the Scriptures call us the Body of Christ. But if, before we could know and wish it, we have been chosen and accepted with the whole Church in Jesus Christ, then we also belong to him in eternity *with* one another. He who looks upon his brother should know that he will be eternally united with him in Jesus Christ. Christian community means community through and in Jesus Christ. (p. 24, emphasis in original)

Consider how Bonhoeffer's argument could change the Becky and Sarah situation. If the roommates come to recognize that they are powerless to change their situation without the love of Christ, efforts to "*win*" the argument become less important. They are bound together because they stand in common relationship to Jesus and His sacrifice. This reality completes the basis of the covenantal relationship described earlier. Because they are bound together "*in Christ*" first and by their college circumstances second, they can begin to see each other as God's gifts presented into their individual lives. They can reach beyond their individual interests to follow a message even better than the one on all the wristbands: "*What DID Jesus Do?*"

Bonhoeffer's observations about the Christological foundations of community combined with Paul's understanding of the Body of Christ add a critical element to the argument being advanced in this book.

Notice that the essence of the Christian University does not depend upon required Bible classes, regular chapel, or prayer before class. It might be reasonable to describe such an institution as faith-based or Christ-centered or Bible-based because these content areas (faith, Christ, Bible) are key to the content delivered in classes. These are all valuable things in their own right, but more is required.

The Christian University is Christian because of the work of Christ in its very midst. As Bonhoeffer observes, the community we experience is not a goal to aim for but a divine reality in our midst, given to us through the sacrificial love of God in Christ through the Holy Spirit:

> Because God has already laid the only foundation for our fellowship, because God has bound us together in one body with other Christians in Jesus Christ, long before we entered into common life with them, we enter into that common life not as demanders but as thankful recipients. (p. 28)

It is Christ in our midst, fulfilling the promise of the Great Commission: "And lo, I am with you always, even to the end of the age" (Matthew 28:20). It is Christ who promised, "wherever two or more are gathered, there am I in your midst" (Matthew 18:20).

7

Making Sense of the World

You're well into the first semester and you're adjusting to the new realities of college life. Not enough sleep, too many social options, too much required reading, last minute papers, and minor interpersonal crises are the order of the day. Just like any recruit to a new organization, you'll find your own path through this maze. Maybe not an ideal path (you will always feel behind and sleep deprived) but it's your own path. That path is an expression of your personal identity but it can also create challenges.

I want you to imagine five students in our freshman class. Each one is a good student attempting to make sense of what is going on in the world of college. (The following examples aren't real but are based on amalgams of situations I've come across over the years).

First, meet Michael. He loves his social problems class. He's had a passion about issues of social justice since he went on an inner-city mission trip in junior high. Learning about factors that shape life for young people in the city has really been wonderful. Also meet Brandon, sitting near him in class, who challenges every fact in the textbook and every assertion made by Dr. Samuels. Brandon believes that people are poor because they are lazy and won't take responsibility for themselves. Michael feels he can't let Brandon keep making such comments. They ran into each other at dinner the other night and the conversation got heated. Some uncomfortable friends helped redirect the conversation to the safer topics of music and sports.

Next, meet Lauren. She grew up in a politically and theologically conservative home. Being homeschooled, she learned early what her parents thought was important. Her literature class is reading Joseph Conrad's *The Heart of Darkness* about an ivory trader in nineteenth- century Africa.

While the theme troubled her at first, she finds that she loves the book. The ideas unpacked in class discussions open some windows she'd never opened before. Arguments about the role of missions and colonialism have begun to bring some real challenge to the positions she's grown up with. The first long break of the semester is coming in a couple of weeks and she's wondering how to talk to her parents about her newfound excitement over the reading material.

Meet Callie. She is entranced by what she's learning in her Old Testament class. She had not realized that what we call "The Bible" is a fascinating collection of oral stories passed down over generations in a culture very different than ours. She has learned that many Old Testament passages must be read in the context of what was happening within Ancient Israel. When visiting her home church this past Sunday, Pastor Moore preached on how Exodus directly reflected our current American experience. She wished Professor Martin were there to help her explain to the pastor why that wasn't an appropriate connection. But she kept her questions to herself and skipped the chance to address them with her folks when they stopped at a restaurant after church.

Next, we have Kevin. He is glad to be at a Christian university. He had selected this school because he was wary of positions held by faculty in secular schools. His biology class was discussing the various approaches Christians have taken to understanding evolution. Kevin was shocked to find that Dr. Simpson refused to treat evolution as one theory among several approaches. Even more astonishing, Dr. Simpson told the class that she had figured out during her graduate training that she could be a Christian and support evolution at the same time. She spent a lot of time discussing a book that NIH Director Francis Collins (Collins, 2006) had written about the process. Kevin has made an appointment to meet with the dean to find out why the university keeps employing a faculty member who doesn't accept a literal reading of Genesis.

The situations faced by our five students are very real. Each of them is in a critical stage of the learning process and they must learn strategies for engaging their individual challenges. Otherwise, they are likely to shut off their critical thinking and simply wait for this particular semester to end.

In order to dissect these examples and provide some general context, we will need to examine the processes of intellectual development that are part of individuation. We'll consider how mental models work to help us see simplicity and how those can be reordered. Finally, we'll consider how to work through the differences we discover.

Stages of Development

We've already looked at the major transition from home and high school to campus and college. I argued that it's the largest transition you've experienced since that first day of kindergarten. We also looked at how changes in modern society have opened up a process of development known as emerging adulthood. The ages of eighteen to twenty-nine are periods of exploration, uncertainty, and impermanence.

There are also some important things happening in the way you process information. Some of this certainly comes from being in new surroundings but others are just part of natural cognitive development: how our process of thinking changes over time. Mentally you aren't the same person you were just seven years ago.[1]

Swiss psychologist Jean Piaget is famous for identifying stages of cognitive development (Berger, 2011). They are:

1. Sensorimotor Stage

2. Preoperational Stage

3. Concrete Operational Stage

4. Formal Operational Stage

An infant is in a sensorimotor stage. In pre-school years, the child is in a preoperational stage, characterized by learning language and learning to perceive perspective. The concrete operational stage characterizes the elementary years, with the child applying more rigid categories and classifications. The teen moves into the formal operations stage and begins to think about abstractions, contrasts, and hypotheticals.

Emory professor James Fowler has applied developmental stages to personal faith. In a ground-breaking work (Fowler, 1981), he articulated the way in which faith changes over time. His stages are:

1. Intuitive Projective Stage

2. Mythic Literal Faith

3. Synthetic Conventional Faith

4. Individuative Reflective Faith

5. Conjunctive Faith

6. Universalizing Faith

1. One of the characteristics of a liberal arts education is that it is designed to stretch you mind. We'll return to this in chapter 9.

Pre-school children express faith through stories with fairly fluid meaning structures. If you've worked with four-year-olds in Sunday school or Vacation Bible School, you've seen this occur. "Jesus" is the answer to any question, but theology can get easily mixed up with Disney princesses! Children through elementary grades adopt what Fowler calls "mythic-literal" approaches to faith. The stories they know are seen as literal models for how the world works. They have a strong sense of reward and punishment.

The third stage, particularly relevant for our purposes, examines the teen years. This period of "synthetic-conventional" faith is characterized by competing motivations. On the one hand, it is a period where obedience to authority is very important. Something said by pastors, youth pastors, parents, and Christian-school teachers trumps other teachers, comments in the media, or patterns in the larger society. On the other hand, this is a period of becoming your own person and working out your own beliefs. While these two poles are often in tension, teens suppress or ignore the tensions in an attempt to hold faith together.

The fourth stage roughly corresponds with the period of emerging adulthood we discussed earlier. In the college years and beyond, the individual expresses what Fowler calls "individuative-reflective" faith. In this period, the pattern of individuation (working out personal beliefs) becomes dominant. One is open to explore new ideas in a search for personal synthesis that makes sense.

Fowler goes on to discuss two more stages occurring in later adulthood. The fifth stage is a "conjunctive" faith that is more comfortable with paradox and openness. It is roughly associated with mid-life issues of the forties. The sixth stage, which Fowler says is very rare, is called "universalizing" faith. This faith approaches all people according to some broad general principles.

One of the difficulties of stage theories is that they suggest general patterns but cannot be directly applied to specific ages. So while I used school transitions as a means of description, we must recognize that each individual progresses at a somewhat different pace. Think back to your high school conversations. Some friends, though eighteen, were processing the world in the same way they did at fourteen. Others were entertaining much more abstract ideas and conversations. (In my long ago high school days, this made for entirely different friendship groups.)

Another challenge to stage models is that they don't adequately deal with the social context of the individual's psychological development.

Growing up in a small town is different than growing up in a suburb or from growing up in the inner city. In some groups, black and white thinking is rewarded and reinforced. Even though a student is of an age that corresponds with formal operational thought, that skill may not get a lot of practice.

Some church groups and some Christian Universities are far more committed to seeing the world in either-or choices while others deal with more complexity and will reinforce mental processes that are more consistent with Piaget's concrete operational stage or Fowler's second and third stages.

For you, at the beginning of your studies at a Christian University, two of the transitions mentioned are particularly significant. The shift from concrete operational to formal operational modes of thinking can be tough. The more you interact with those from different backgrounds or read challenging material, the harder it is to maintain rigid categories. Similarly, moving from the quiet acceptance of Fowler's second stage to the questing of the third stage is a point of reordering one's thought patterns and literally thinking in new ways about faith and the world. It may seem as if you are "losing your faith" but it is far more likely that you are, perhaps for the first time, thinking seriously about what you really believe.

Rachel Held Evans is a popular Christian author (she has nearly twenty-five thousand twitter followers!). Her first book, *Evolving in Monkey Town* (2010), illustrates the challenges the Piaget and Fowler transitions predict. Her subtitle underscores the transitions well: How a Girl Who Knew All the Answers Learned to Ask Questions. Rachel grew up around Christian university campuses and went to Christian high school, summer camps, and mission trips. She was an expert at apologetics.[2] She knew all the answers one was supposed to give. But a series of events in the midst of her college years required that she start asking questions for herself. The easy answers were replaced by a sense of confusion and uncertainty. She was still active on campus and served as student body president, but inside she was doing the hard work of making sense of things for herself. Ten years later, she's still doing that hard work.

Let's revisit a couple of our students from the beginning of this chapter with Piaget and Fowler's transitions in mind. Our first scenario involved

---

2. Apologetics is an approach to defending Christian faith through the use of predetermined categories of theological answers.

Michael and Brandon disagreeing in their social problems class. Why is Michael so open to the issues in the class while Brandon seems so opposed?

While there may be many factors involved in answering this question (family upbringing, political orientation, etc.) I want to focus more carefully on Piaget's stages. Brandon is more likely to still be operating in a concrete operational form of thought while Michael is operating in the formal operational stage.

Brandon finds past classification systems easy to understand and uses anecdotal information to buttress those prior ways of thinking. The class may be discussing the vast differences between achievement in inner-city and suburban school systems and how those reflect economic or policy decisions. But Brandon is most likely to raise an objection based on the story of that one guy who quit school because being a drug lookout was more lucrative. Brandon is not likely to ask himself important questions, such as: How representative is that story? What details might be missing? How does that one person's story relate to the broader discussion?

Michael, on the other hand, has been on inner-city mission trips and has experience interacting with the people who live there. He has the capacity to imagine what it's like to live in that environment, to construct a hypothetical model that takes him out of his suburban environment and mentally puts him into the inner-city world. He quickly grasps the abstraction of how economic inequality might lead to residential segregation and further inequality.

Let me take a moment to be very clear. I'm not celebrating Michael for taking a "liberal" position and critiquing Brandon for taking a "conservative" approach. Brandon might well argue that more public spending on education is counterproductive. What is at issue here is not WHAT Brandon and Michael are arguing for but HOW they are presenting their cases. In most situations, their classroom "discussions" will be highly frustrating because they aren't just talking about facts and policies but are engaged in differences in how they think about the world.

Our second scenario is about Lauren's literature class. Her reading has her celebrating the "liberal arts" in the classical sense—she's seeing things about herself she never saw before and becoming "free." But it's hard because it challenges her homeschooling, her family background, and her church community. They didn't read "those kinds of books" in her home. Yet, not only is she reading those kinds of books, but she loves them.

Fowler's faith stages help us interpret what's happening in Lauren's mind and heart. Her upbringing is particularly well matched with a conventional-synthetic faith. She and her family placed a high value on believing in a certain way. Books, studies, family trips, and church style reinforced their mode of belief. Because she loves her family and her church, Lauren values their judgment. Respecting her parents' judgment and conforming to authority is highly important.

What does she do with her feelings about her books? In the conventional-synthetic stage, she is trying to stay open to her own ideas but also wants to support her parents. Managing that conflict is difficult and personally costly. But over the next few years, she will increasingly be making choices on her own and reconciling those choices to her personal faith. As she moves into the individuative-reflective stage, she'll find ways of better articulating her own approach to finding faith through literature. We'll come back to how she articulates this new understanding a little later.

Thinking about thinking

Piaget and Fowler (along with many others) give us some convenient handles for how our thought processes change over time. Work by cognitive social psychologists provides some additional points of reference as we make sense of the world around us.

In fact, the idea of "making sense" sets cognitive approaches apart from other branches of psychology. Behaviorism, for example, isn't particularly concerned about why something happens. It is far more interested in the process of training responses to particular stimuli. Social scientists working from a cognitive framework have a presumption that we want our world to fit together.

Think back to when you first arrived on campus. If you're like most students (not counting those with siblings at the school), a good description of your mental world was overwhelmed. All those people to meet! Where are your classes? Which food is best in the cafeteria? Which rules are most important to attend to? How do you navigate the Blackboard system to do your assignments? How can you keep track of all the campus events? What's the difference between your RA and your spiritual advisor and whom do you go to when?

Now that's just creepy

Today it's hard to imagine that you ever felt disoriented. You know where to go, when to eat lunch, whom to hang with, and how to ask for help when you need it. What changed?

Social psychologists observe that you make sense of your environment using what we call schemas: "*mental structures that help us organize information*" (Baron, Byrne, & Branscombe, 2007). You can think of schemas as being like the file folders on a computer. When you see something familiar, you know it goes in that particular file. (If you don't organize your documents in folders, you should start now.) If you come in contact with some new experience, you try to make it fit into the folder that comes closest.

When you came to college, you found mental shortcuts that allowed you to figure things out. Most likely, it happened as you thought, "this class is a lot like my English class last year" or "the girl down the hall reminds me of that one girl at camp." Other things get ingrained in a short period of time through simple repetition; i.e., you always eat lunch at the same time and start at the salad bar and you always sit in the second row on the left in psychology class.

Schemas shape what we pay attention to and what we remember. The less something fits an established folder, the more likely we'll notice it or remember it. This error makes it seem like our expectations were met because we're discounting things that don't fit.

Sometimes those substitute folders are completely wrong. That girl is nothing like that girl at camp. In fact, in two weeks you won't be able to figure out what you thought the similarity was in the first place. Or, you didn't understand what your professor wanted for that first paper because his expectations were very different from your English teacher last year.

We're in a bind. We need the schemas to orient ourselves, but there's a real risk of error. We operate through a series of successive estimations, learning through trial and error what fits and what needs to be adjusted.

Schemas can help us make sense of Callie's story. She is enjoying her Old Testament class a lot, but finds that she must rework some of her prior schemas. The folders she used in Sunday School and Youth Group aren't adequate to organize what she's learned about the Bible in these few short weeks. She has decided to approach the material from an open stance and not a closed one, so she's willing to restructure some of her mental file folders. She still has a folder called Bible, but it's got a lot more complexity in its organization than before. There are lots of subfolders and links between them.

When she heard the pastor making comments about Exodus, she was aware that the comment didn't fit her new schemas. Pastor Moore has likely made similar comments before but Callie didn't notice. Now she not only notices, but also wants to reconcile the comment with her understanding. In Fowler's terms, she's in the conventional-synthetic stage, so authority figures like the pastor are important. However, it's not necessary for her to decide whether Pastor Moore or Professor Martin "wins." What is important is that Callie finds ways of organizing her schemas that acknowledge differences of background and purpose.

Callie's example helps illustrate the complexity of perceiving our surroundings. We are continuously sorting, evaluating, and restructuring inputs. That's hard work. It requires an awareness of new perspectives, new information, changing contexts, and personal growth. Sometimes it's just too much to manage.

Social psychology suggests that one way we deal with information overload is by using heuristics: *"simple rules for making complex decisions or drawing inferences in a rapid and efficient manner"* (Baron et al., 2007). If schemas are the file folders in your computer, heuristics are the means you use to review those folders on a regular basis.

Here's a simple example. My twitter account keeps me updated on a wide variety of people or news sites. Most of those sites contain links to other stories that might be interesting. But if I decided to explore the link on every tweet, I'd never get this book written (I'm not as focused as some!). So I have some higher-order means of making decisions about which tweets to attend to. For example, there are a handful of evangelical writers I'm building relationship with. If I see a tweet from one of them, I'll stop and look because it's personal. If the tweet is about a topic of general interest to me, I'll invest a little more time. Most twitter feeds just slide past me without even registering significantly in my memory. They don't even make my mental file folders.

My example helps illustrate how we create shortcuts for making sense of the world around us. We quickly categorize information and act accordingly. Heuristics are not foolproof, however. Often, we wind up trading ease of information processing for accuracy. The two rules I use for twitter (relationships and interest) can actually keep me from learning. My relationship rule means that I won't benefit from new people whose views might differ from mine. My interest rule means that my thinking gets narrow and my attempts to know what's happening really lead me to continuing to plow the same field.

If I've already got some clear positions on a topic, I'm going to be more attentive to those tweets that affirm my position or are so far removed that I can dismiss them. It takes real effort to break through the clutter to see what else might be going on.

Ken Bain, in his book *What the Best College Students Do* (2012), explores how mental processes like heuristics inhibit learning for some students, but not for the best ones:

> I have had students in my U.S. history class who entered the course with almost religious convictions about what they thought happened in the past. When they encountered new evidence that suggested other histories, they couldn't bring themselves to consider it. In contrast, the people in our study cared deeply about their own education, found the world fascinating and endlessly exciting, and became enthralled with discovery as part of their personal quest to grow their own minds. Finding a new way of thinking didn't bother them. Indeed, they became intrigued with different concepts that would let them see some familiar objects or situations in a whole new way. (p. 69)

One of the "best students" Bain interviewed was comedian and satirist Stephen Colbert. Colbert uses Jesus' caution in the Sermon on the Mount to "worry about nothing" as guidance when dealing with the unknown. That includes the important ability to risk failure and to learn from the experience.

Colbert's example would be helpful for our fifth student scenario: Kevin's issue with his biology class. Remember, Kevin was quite concerned to learn that Dr. Simpson found compatibility between Christianity and evolution.

What is the basis for Kevin's concern? In all likelihood, his worries about his professor holding a positive view of evolution is a sign that evolution is operating as a shorthand or heuristic for a lot of other things.

There are scientists who try to explain human origins as simple matters of chance or natural occurrence. There are those who see religion as simple superstition. But the majority of scientists don't fall into such extreme camps. In my experience, you can't find a single science faculty member in a Christian university who denies the role of a Creator God even if she leaves the process for creation open.

For students like Kevin, the heuristic simply shuts down the ability to think creatively. If he could remove the fear or worry from the situation, as

Colbert suggests, he'd be open to exploring new ideas and seeing how they might fit existing schemas. In fact, if Kevin were to sit down over lunch with Dr. Simpson in order to hear her story, the odds are very high that she has a lot to say about how her schemas reorganized as she learned more about biological processes. She was able to find arrangements of her own mental file folders that allowed her to be a Christian biologist in a rich and meaningful way.

In our Christian conversations, heuristics often show up in "slippery slope" arguments. If we don't hold the line on A, then B will follow, C will happen next, and so forth. These are shorthand mechanisms for organizing information to provide security in a complex world. If your initial reaction to new information is one of fear, you may be running up against a heuristic. But remember to hear Jesus' words of comfort that Colbert clung to. You aren't alone in your search. The Spirit of God is present in the very midst of your reading.

This is the lesson we saw in Peter's vision. Mosaic law called for him to act in specific ways and avoid anything unclean. His initial response to the vision of the sheet was a heuristic response. But he listened to God's leading and found new ways of understanding (as did the other disciples).

I've set these scenarios early in the school year to introduce the challenges of personalizing and strengthening the schemas you use to make sense of the world around you. But the adjustment to new ideas and experiences isn't just something associated with beginning your college years. You want your remaining years in college or graduate school to do more of the same. You want your first jobs to be places of learning and internalization of new lessons. And you want it all to make sense.

Sharon Daloz Parks writes provocatively about meaning-making for emerging adults:

> It is my conviction that the central work of the young adult era in the cycle of human life is not located in any of these tasks or circumstances [of life]. Rather, the promise and vulnerability of young adulthood lie in the experience of the birth of critical awareness and the dissolution and recomposition of the meaning of self, other, world, and "God." This work has enormous consequences for the years of adulthood to follow. Young adulthood is rightfully a time of asking big questions and discovering worthy dreams. (Parks, 2000, 5)

Parks characterizes the first transition from home and family to independence as a move from authority to relativism. This is where you may be at the beginning of college. There is a vast array of ideas and perspectives and you're trying to find your place. But she points out that the relativism is short-lived, giving way to what she calls "probing commitment." This is replaced in the thirties with "tested commitment" and eventually with "convictional commitment" (2000, p. 69).

It is probing commitment that best matches the college experience. In fact, it is the unifying theme between all four of our student scenarios. Michael and Brandon, Lauren, Callie, and Kevin are all asking good questions about the new world in which they find themselves. I think it's important to notice that Parks sees the relativistic phase as short-lived. The real focus is on how you make sense of what you're learning.

"Probing" also says something about the method through which you do your sense-making. It is the process of looking at a variety of ideas and testing them against your existing schemas. Notice that this is not about proving or coming to final answers. That comes later in life.

For this period of life, your purpose is to explore, question, wonder, discuss, argue, challenge, and test. There is something immensely liberating (as in liberal arts) about the probing stance. It means that you aren't required to have all the answers or even be sure about the questions.

Ideally, your professors have made sufficient space in class for you to ask questions like "what if . . ." "does that imply . . . ," "but what about . . . ," "how does this connect . . ." These questions are far more significant to your development of probing commitment than "do we have to know . . . ," or "what was point two?" We'll come back to learning and teaching in a later chapter in order to push the probing a little further.

Engaging Differences

The notion of probing brings us to a final point for this chapter. How do we engage those who differ from us? How should Michael talk to Brandon (and vice versa)? What about Lauren and her parents or Callie and Pastor Moore? How can Kevin have a productive conversation with Dr. Simpson?

First, remember that this stage of life is more about good questions than solid answers. There's plenty of time to get to convictions and if you trust the leading of the Spirit, there is no fear in exploring ideas. We're often tempted to share our positions on things when we really need to be sharing our ponderings. Michael and Brandon might have had an excellent dinner conversation about their upbringing, travels, and the questions they may have about different styles of life. By interacting as persons and not advocates for positions, there is a chance that new understandings might lead to surprising commonalities.

Second, realize that even your questions have tentativeness about them. Lauren isn't just struggling with how Conrad's *Heart of Darkness* is opening up new ideas, she isn't even sure she can accurately form the questions she wants to ask her parents. A better option is to simply describe what she's reading and why she finds it interesting. In the process, she will likely discover that her parents had their own challenging moments with things they read or events that unfolded. If the conversation is about new insights and the process of learning and not "this is not how you raised me," it will lead to some very interesting places.

Third, there is value in really listening to others. If Callie sat down with Pastor Moore, she might learn a great deal about his own background and what his specific intent was in what he said about Exodus. It may be that he misspoke on a relatively minor point in his sermon. It may be that he was trying to address a larger concern and did it awkwardly. In any case, she should avoid a rapid judgment. Comparing Pastor Moore and Dr. Martin isn't fair because they're speaking to different audiences with different objectives.

Fourth, in all cases avoid litmus tests: shorthand yes or no questions designed to trap a respondent. Beginning with some proposition about "what real Christians believe" isn't going to lead to new answers. It is far more interested in drawing lines in the sand. If we take Kevin's statements at face value, he doesn't want to understand Dr. Simpson; he wants her fired. Callie has to be careful not to label Pastor Moore as an anti-intellectual leader who should be ignored. Michael has to make sure that he doesn't just call Brandon heartless because he doesn't agree with a progressive sociologist (and Brandon needs to avoid using a socialist label to describe Michael).

There are many more practical lessons we could explore about how to take a light-handed approach to important questions. The simplified definition is to keep our positions relatively open while seeking to maintain our own authenticity and the identity of others.

I was reminded of these practical lessons when reading the Brennan Manning' memoir *All is Grace* (2010) about his struggles with alcoholism.

At one point, he spends time at a rehab facility in Minnesota. While at the facility, he was given a worksheet to evaluate how seriously he was taking the group work. I share it here because it can be easily adapted to how we deal with new questions or differences of opinion. It's what avoiding probing commitment looks like.

1. I don't see you participating in group without prodding
2. I hear you trying to patch everyone up in the community
3. I see you feeling that you deserve special treatment
4. I hear you talking down to other patients in the unit
5. I see you full of denial (minimizing, explaining, justifying)
6. I see you hiding in anger
7. I see you acting like an "old pro" in treatment
8. I see you playing counselor
9. I see you being self-controlled
10. I see you trying to manage the unit
11. I see you not accepting your addiction
12. I hear you bragging about your addiction (war stories)
13. I hear you talking one way in group and another way in community (pp. 121–22)

I would substitute educational terms for group intervention terms. I'd say that each of these problems that inhibit growing in group treatment also keep a student from engaging the kinds of questions that lead to the construction of useful meaning structures (schemas and heuristics).

Manning says he violated every one of these guidelines. He put in his required time in group, but it didn't do him much good. Furthermore, it was harmful to the others in the group because his stubbornness kept others from getting what they needed.

I could create a list like Manning's to describe students who are present in class but not engaged.

1. I see you coming to class without reading
2. I see you holding back contributions to class so you won't "look smart"
3. I hear you disrespecting your professor and classmates
4. I hear you making excuses rather than engaging

5. I see you grasping entitlement as a customer rather than engaging as a learner

If our five students avoid the hard work of making sense of their educational experiences, they are reduced to simply putting in the required time to earn a credit on a transcript. Like Brennan, they meet minimal expectations, but they don't do themselves, or others, much good in the process. It will be much harder to move toward Park's convictional commitment down the road. And they will keep others from progressing as well.

What's the alternative? Throw yourself into the questions. Know that you are surrounded by others who are also on a journey of meaning: fellow students, professors, even your parents. Don't rush to get to answers. Probe the options. Develop tentative conclusions but be willing to adjust them in the face of new information.

And finally, realize that you aren't alone. Just as God spoke to Peter in ways that allowed him to make sense of what he was learning, God is also speaking to you. If you listen and act, you'll be helping with the creation of God's kingdom on Earth.

8

It's All About Learning

We left Michael and Brandon considering how they might get along in their social problems class. They have different views and perhaps even different ways of thinking. In this chapter we need to take a deeper look at what learning means within their Christian university. How will they help others build community without destroying their identity? What can they do to make the most of their time in college that will adequately prepare them for all the uncertainties of life beyond graduation?

Chapter 2 reviewed four reasons why Michael and Brandon might have chosen a Christian college or university: to get a job, to be in a safe environment, to take the next step in an educational journey, and to find who they are. All are important, but the last one is most important. The first three provide support, but not a lot of projection into the future. In this chapter, we'll look more deeply into what contributes to personal development during the college years.

Here's the short version of the argument. You hold the keys to learning. Learning isn't about stuff you are told; it's about putting the pieces together to better understand yourself, others, society, and God. You will do that in unique ways suited to you. You will do that by affirming the unique learning processes of those around you. In short, you will be part of a community of learners making each other smarter and more grace filled, able to navigate complexity, and celebrating intellectual humility.

The job orientation won't do that because instead of being about the kind of person who will live out your personal story it's focused on finding the skills needed for the first position. The safe Christian environment is incomplete precisely because of the transition out of that environment coming in a few short years. The bureaucratic "next step" approach makes education about collecting tickets to a credential.

A celebration of learning, on the other hand, looks at all circumstances as having the potential to spark Spirit-led change. This is why I said that Reason was the method of connecting Wesley's themes of Scripture, Tradition, and Experience. Your celebration of learning has the potential of enriching every class you attend. It can bring out the best in those around you. It can help engage a changing society through the message of God's grace.

Too much of American education has focused on the job and bureaucratic approach. Too much of Christian higher education has been about being separate: sometimes at real cost to deep thinking and intellectual rigor. That means you need to be open to some new thinking about learning. Your past models aren't developed enough for your current situation. Discovering the models that work for you today can be scary. But that's okay because you aren't going through this journey on your own.

Critiquing Higher Education

Many people critique higher education in today's society. Journalists worry about college debt, tuition pricing, or graduates living with their parents while working at McDonald's. Some scholars have focused more directly on the problems of learning. Their concerns are worth our attention.

In 2011, a single book seemed to turn the higher education world upside down. Two sociologists, Richard Arum and Joseph Roksa reported on a major research project about student learning in *Academically Adrift* (Arum & Roksa, 2011). They had used a new measure of student learning, the Collegiate Learning Assessment (CLA), to see what students really learned during the first two years of college,[1] especially as it related to the development of critical thinking. The results were shocking:

> With a large sample of 2,300 students, we observe no statistically significant gains in critical thinking, complex reasoning, and writing skills for at least 45 percent of the students in our study. (p. 36)

They do point out that students have gained "subject-specific" knowledge. However, there are solid reasons to believe that those gains are

---

1. This was selected because many schools put all of their "general education" courses in the first two years.

somewhat short-lived. Arum and Roksa attempted to find out what kinds of experiences were common among those who did better than average on CLA gains. They found that students who were asked to read seventy-five pages a week or who had to write twenty pages a semester for their classes did seem to score higher (this is only relational data and doesn't tell us about cause and effect).

When those expectations are put alongside the recent data on the time students report studying for classes, their findings make some intuitive sense. A recent Washington Post review (de Vise, 2012) shows how study patterns have changed over time with students reporting an average of fifteen hours studying per week, down nine hours from the 1960s. The review does a good job explaining some of the contributing factors: more students working, technological enhancements make paper writing and research easier, and increased volunteerism. Still, doing minimums at the last minute for an assignment or test is consistent with too much of what we've been reviewing in terms of college life.

Richard Keeling and Richard Hersh are educational consultants who wrote a remarkable little book that provides a way forward from the critiques we've been examining. In *We're Losing Our Minds* (Keeling & Hersh, 2011), they examine what neurophysiologists are learning about brain function. They distinguish between "*ordinary, pedestrian*" learning that depends on cramming and memorization from "*higher learning, which demands engagement and inspires positive, beneficial growth and change.*" The latter actually changes the structure of the brain function. The former does not. It's an interesting approach to provide new meaning to the phrase "higher" education.

Keeling and Hersh go on to examine how we'd change assignments and the nature of the campus environment if we were to put such higher learning at the center of what we do. Their critique is blunt:

> The current culture of colleges and universities no longer puts learning first—and in most institutions that culture perpetuates a fear of doing so. (p. 154)

It's hard to change a culture. It is far easier to go along with what's been before. "If it ain't broke, don't fix it," the adage goes. But it may be that we're simply pretending it isn't broke because that's easier than fixing it. You see if we focus on your learning and keep that in the center of what we do together, it changes the entire dynamic of the university.

Now, I don't think this critique is really about students like you. I quickly tire of the "what's the matter with kids today" complaint. Your generation is simply the one that grew up with No Child Left Behind. We've been testing you and re-testing you. We've written report cards on your schools and evaluated how much you learned over a set period of time. The challenges in higher education started much earlier.

I started college over forty years ago. As I explained earlier, my transition to college was full of roadblocks. I felt lost and overwhelmed. I got behind in my coursework and did minimums on what I did finish. Looking back, I was certainly a victim of the bureaucratic form of college attendance. I went through the motions with what I thought others wanted me to do.

All those legislators, journalists, and television pundits complaining about higher education didn't flunk out of college like I did, but there's little evidence that they grasped the centrality of learning. Their tendency to make facile arguments is testimony to their lack of complex thinking.

When I went back to school after flunking out, I changed my orientation from the simple bureaucratic approach to being engaged in my learning. It took a little while but I began seeing my classes as an opportunity for learning. Even in the ones I wasn't nuts about, I found that I could engage my long-term interests through the course material. Building quality relationships with my faculty was an outgrowth of that quest.

I've tried to make clear that I hope you will put personal learning at the center of all that you do with your college years. It's far better to let the job search take care of itself[2] and to resist the bureaucratic impulse to simply go through the motions. That was the message my friend was giving regarding the importance of "forty-one classes in Larry."

So we've got Michael and Brandon in their social problems class. We need to explore what it means for them to put learning in the center. That learning encompasses all of the university experience: in class, in the residence hall, on the internship, on the volleyball court, in chapel. Everything is about the learning.

2. The Association of American Colleges and Universities (AAC&U) has regularly conducted surveys of employers regarding what they want in new hires. Invariably, the employers want creative thinkers who communicate well, who have a solid set of ethical values, and who exercise imagination in problem solving. Develop those habits and the jobs will come.

Learning in the College Classroom

It is a curious fact that most of college education occurs outside of the official classroom. Students do their reading, their accounting problems, and their papers during "their" time, not class time. Similarly, the professor is preparing presentations, writing exams, and grading exams and papers on "his" or "her" time. Successful completion of those activities can be rewarded with grades and credits in the permanent record that can lead to the awarding of a degree.

We pay insufficient attention to the assumptions of what ought to occur during those periods in class, the part of the experience that exists in our "shared" time. The average four-year college student will spend 1,860 hours sitting in the classroom.[3] While this is a minority of the total time invested in education (see the chart below), it is still a significant part of one's life. If those hours were spent in one sitting (a thought too horrific to imagine), the student would be sitting in that classroom for over seventy-seven days straight! When classroom time is compared to other alternative uses of that same time, it demands that the return on investment is worthwhile. (It is this very calculation that causes some students to struggle with class attendance.)

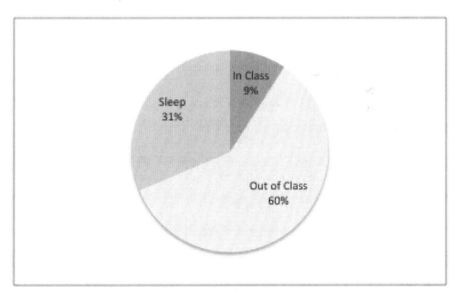

3. The chart makes the following assumptions. The student is taking fifteen and a half credits per fifteen week semester for eight semesters and averaging seven and a half hours of sleep per night.

Let's return to Ken Bain's research on "what the best college students do" (Bain, 2012). There are some general patterns in Bain's students that will help Michael, Brandon, and their classmates put learning at the center of university life.

Bain and his colleagues set out to interview people who have led extraordinary lives. Not content to simply take the next bureaucratic step or to look for the next job, these are people of creativity and accomplishment. They invented things. They paved new paths. They broke molds. In the interviews, they asked the subjects to reflect on their key lessons from their college days. What set them apart was actually not a set of talents or experiences, but an overall orientation to learning:

> They pursued the development of the dynamic power of the mind, and that end—not academic honors or simply surviving college— became their primary goal . . . [They] came to understand themselves better and out of those insights to appreciate the unique qualities and experiences that they could bring to any project. In turn, the more they understood about themselves, the greater confidence they had, and the more they appreciated the special qualities and achievements of everyone else. They became students of other people's histories—in the sciences, humanities, and arts. Most important, they found a way to motivate themselves to work. (Bain, 2012, p. 5)

Michael and Brandon need to grasp three things here. First, the educational experience will require them to incorporate their learning into "what makes them tick." In other words, they will internalize the information as part of a larger project of self-discovery. In their particular case, it means understanding *why* they react so differently to the social problems class. There are aspects of their experiences and thought processes that make them unique. They need to own these but also treat them as objects to be carefully (even critically) examined.

Second, Bain suggests that knowing the connections between your sense of self and what you learn increases confidence. You aren't reciting something the text said or repeating what some teacher commented in class. The text and the comment are both fair game for understanding, but the connection to self means you can articulate why you advocate for a certain position. Michael and Brandon have very different experiences with poverty but those experiences become lenses for engaging the course material rather than pre-determined conclusions.

Third, in ways that are consistent with the themes of the last two chapters, Bain's learners knew that the discovery of difference is not the end of some process of "finding oneself" but the beginning of a long, collaborative journey. Understanding oneself is the first step. The more important steps are using the knowledge to better comprehend others and to work together to deepen understandings through the leading of the Holy Spirit.

Earlier I quoted Parker Palmer: "Truth is between us, in relationship, to be found in the dialogue of knowers and knowns who are understood as independent but accountable selves" (Palmer, 1993). I have come to take Palmer's image quite literally—when I think of Truth being between us I imagine the spot on the classroom floor that exists exactly between us. If, for example, we created a graph of all twelve students in a class plus their professor, there is only one place that is equidistant between all of them. That's the place where we must focus.

Let me offer an illustration on how this works. I remember a conversation with a faculty colleague. She was teaching a class in human sexuality to adult students. She started the class with a confidential attitude and a behavior survey that would help her plan her classroom presentations and discussions most effectively. When she got the results compiled, she found that the class had great disparities in experiences and polar opposition in attitudes. My colleague questioned how she could possibly teach this group of students while maintaining the safe environment needed for discussing a sensitive topic in a constructive manner.

This human sexuality class is different in that most classes do not begin with the survey that brought the sharp distinctions to light in the first place. In that sense, my colleague was more aware of the potential challenges present in her class than other professors might have been in their classes. And yet I would argue that it is incumbent on the professor to quickly get a read on the diversity present in the classroom, because it will inevitably be as important a factor in the success of the class as the professor's deep background reading and magnificent PowerPoint presentations.

We discovered that the secret to making the most of the experience was to make the diversity the key educational method of the course. By walking into class and presenting the survey results, my colleague was able to do two things. First, she got the diversity into everyone's consciousness and kept each student from only viewing the class through a specific set of lenses and assuming everyone else was just like he or she was. Second, my colleague's role shifted from simply presenting information to helping move the class toward a common and respectful appreciation of the subject material. The secret to the change in role rested in her ability to be completely honest about the challenge she faced in teaching in the face of the diversity. In that honesty, she was bringing her unfolding story as a teacher into the midst of the class itself. The class was not simply about human sexuality any longer but was now about how this particular group of people (including the professor) can study human sexuality together, given what they knew about each other. This significantly shifted the class from being "about" sexuality to having the possibility of being an opportunity for personal growth both individually and collectively.

It would be nice if I could tell you that a common understanding was the inevitable result of their joint experience but I'm sure that's an exaggeration. The class was only seven weeks long and anyone can suppress their disagreements for such a short time (the pseudocommunity described in chapter 6). Factionalism between the conservatives and liberals, with little attempt at mediation, is also a short-term political resolution. Still, I think the story of this class provides important clues about how the classroom would ideally operate.

Back to Michael and Brandon's social problems class. It's not just Dr. Samuels' responsibility to acknowledge the diversity. It's incumbent on Michael, Brandon, and their thirty classmates to figure out how to work through their experiences in ways that deepen their understandings while valuing each person's uniqueness.

Some might suggest that my approach is so individually oriented that the only solution is to accept each person as he or she is, which leads to an extreme form of relativism. But my point is exactly the opposite. I affirm that each individual is in a different spot but that there is an ultimate understanding that will emerge with time. It is likely to occur at some point in the future, maybe when the student's children are beginning college. But if the Holy Spirit is leading us to new understandings, it is hard to see how relativism is possible.

If we take a life-long approach to education, then the classroom is not about the material to be studied. It is the environment where all of the individual understandings come together to teach everyone, students and professors alike, something remarkably new. Returning to the words of Palmer, the academic classroom is a *"space where the community of truth is practiced"* (1993).

I'll be honest. Taking this approach to the classroom scares me as a faculty member. Remember, I'm a Scarecrow. I like brains. I believe there are particular topics everyone should know in sociology because those topics have fascinated me my whole life. I am good at the traditional information-based academic game. I know how to summarize articles and build them into the arguments I want to make. I think I'm good at "looking smart." I organize my classroom to maximize my strengths and keep a strong sense of control over what happens.

If the classroom becomes about students exploring the connections between their past experiences, unique strengths, and understanding of the course material, it becomes uncontrollable. We would never know exactly where today's class would take us. I'd have to get much more comfortable saying "I never looked at it that way." Students would have to confront differences, not in an attempt to win an argument but in the pursuit of truth.

In the short term, it would complicate my life. In the long run, it would bring out the beauty of lives transformed. The work would be hard but the potential rewards are immense. If only a third of the people reading these words took them to heart and began to practice them in class, we'd completely revolutionize the Christian university.

We already saw that your generation has a heightened tolerance for risk-taking. So take the risk. Upset the apple cart. We'll all have a more meaningful educational experience as a result.

Learning Outside the Classroom

If it is true that a student spends 1,860 hours over four years in a college classroom, that leaves nearly 12,000 non-sleeping hours unaccounted for (even more if all-nighters are considered).[4] You spend this remaining time on homework, naps, jobs, athletic practice, intramurals, socializing, movie nights, service activities, video games, ministry opportunities, family, dating, political activism, shopping, student organizations, and many other possible activities.

It's curious that nearly all of the Hollywood renditions of college involve the non-classroom part of life. There are too many instances to recount. Let me share a general plotline. Sally is a new student at Major University and meets all these diverse people on her floor. They are a mix of personality types and ethnicities. Life involves a series of parties, conflicts,

---

4. The earlier chart shows this as sixty percent of the student's time.

and relationships (sometimes all at the same time). Alcohol and sexual in-vitations are present at every turn. You rarely see students go to class and never see them working on the paper due the next day.

In this image, social life is the *real* part of college and classes are what one does to stay in the residence hall. We keep telling you that you'll make life-long friends at school, right?

Academics and social life are seen as two spheres that frequently con-flict. This is the plotline of Tom Wolfe's *I Am Charlotte Simmons* (2004). It's not the best rendition of college life but it does illustrate the challenges of the two spheres. Charlotte is a prodigious student from the hills of North Carolina who is admitted to prestigious Dupont University. She loves her classes but is soon caught up in all the intrigues of the social world: parties, boyfriends, helping boyfriend with papers, parties, sex, athletics, and par-ties. At the end of the story (700 pages later), Charlotte has succeeded in transforming from a shy small town girl to the basketball star's girlfriend. But she's failed academically.

Here's where the television shows, movies, and novels go wrong. *They fail to see that all aspects of university life contribute to a student's learning.* The lessons of the classroom are replicated in the lessons in the residence hall or on the baseball diamond. The lessons of how to get along in a small group Bible study are the same lessons needed to complete that big eco-nomics project.

Seymour Hersh identifies this interdependence as key to a success-ful, residential liberal arts experience. As a college president, he knew the dynamic environment necessary for learning:

> The best education takes place at the nexus of profound intel-lectual and social/emotional development. Yet most colleges and universities dichotomize the various facets of learning, as if our intellectual, emotional, and ethical lives were compartmentalized. This paradigm of compartmentalized learning is extended to "life" on most campuses—faculty take care of the intellect, student ser-vices staff and coaches[5] handle the rest. What goes on inside the classroom is thought of as separate and different from what takes place outside. One of higher education's fundamental tasks, and the modus operandi of liberal arts colleges, is to undo such false dichotomies and foster a more global or holistic version of educa-tion. (Hersh, 2000, p. 182)

---

5. I referred to these as "tin men" in the Wizard of Oz chapter.

How do we undo this dichotomy to see learning active in all interactions? The secret lies in working through the issues of diversity and community in all settings in which we find ourselves. Let's look at some more sources of diversity and explore how those lead to learning.

Howard Gardner and his colleagues at Harvard argue that what we regularly call "*intelligence*" is but a limited view of how we relate to the world (Gardner, 1993). Our normal use of intelligence relies disproportionately on verbal and mathematical abilities. Instead of these important but limited approaches to intelligence, Gardner suggests that there may be at least eight types of intelligence. Each approach suggests a unique set of mechanisms allowing the individual to solve problems in their lives. This is an important point: The key factor is how one solves problems, not simply what one "*knows*."

Gardner's eight types of intelligence can be briefly summarized as follows:

1. Linguistic (manipulates words and symbols)

2. Logical-mathematical (mathematical patterns)

3. Spatial (relationship between objects)

4. Musical (understanding tone, phrasing, etc.)

5. Bodily-kinesthetic (physical activity)

6. Natural intelligence (related to science and nature)

7. Interpersonal intelligence (works through issues in interaction)

8. Intrapersonal intelligence (works through issues by "going within")

Each of these represents a unique method of problem solving. For example, a student with bodily-kinesthetic intelligence will solve problems using movement or sports metaphors. One strong in interpersonal intelligence (like me) solves problems by talking them through with a somewhat willing listener. Another person strong in intrapersonal intelligence will solve problems by getting alone to consider the variety of solutions possible.

This is not the same as skill or interest. A person may have a strong sense of linguistic intelligence without writing well. A person may be outgoing or extroverted without using interpersonal intelligence to solve problems.

Each of us has specific intelligences while we lack others. If people examined their two strongest forms of intelligence and their two weakest forms, there are seventy different combinations possible. In other words, it is possible to interact with sixty-nine other people before you found someone with exactly the same combinations that you have.

Of course, in practice, things are not this random. Fellow members of the soccer team are likely to share a high sense of bodily-kinesthetic intelligence. People in student government are likely to have a higher sense of interpersonal intelligence.

The importance of Gardner's approach is that it recognizes the tremendous complexity of the individuals involved in an educational institution or any other setting:

> It is of the utmost importance that we recognize and nurture all of the varied human intelligences, and all of the combinations of intelligences. We are all so different largely because we all have different combinations of intelligences. If we recognize this, I think we will have at least a better chance of dealing appropriately with the many problems that we face in the world. If we can mobilize the spectrum of human abilities, not only will people feel better about themselves and more competent: it is even possible that they will also feel more engaged and better able to join the rest of the world community in working for the broader good. Perhaps if we can mobilize the full range of human intelligences and ally them to an ethical sense, we can help to increase the likelihood of our survival on this planet and perhaps even contribute to our thriving. (1993, p. 12)

Gardner is suggesting that we are each different and it is precisely these differences that become tools for learning. Individuals or groups see the world in different ways because of the different methods they use to solve problems.

A couple of chapters back we met two new roommates: Sarah and Becky. We considered that their very different backgrounds require them to navigate Peck's community stages if they are to be successful over the long run. Gardner's perspective adds another layer to their story. Let's suppose that Becky is a science major. She's loved the outdoors her whole life and can tell you all about the difference between different kinds of rock formations. The natural world just "makes sense" to her. Sarah is an English major and loves to write. She expresses herself through words. In fact, she learns what she thinks by writing.[6] Gardner is suggesting that their brains actually

---

6. A trait she shares with the author.

work differently. If they learn from each other's approach to intelligence, they'll be stronger friends. It will also become invaluable when Sarah takes a class in geology and Becky takes American Lit.

In 2002, Donald Clifton and Charles "Chip" Anderson suggested that each of us has unique strengths that set us apart from others. They define strength as being an individual talent that is enhanced with specific knowledge and skills. Their approach has been valuable to colleges across the country.

Their method is a refinement of three decades of leadership research by the Gallup organization. Individuals have what they call "*signature themes*." They define a signature theme as providing insight into a "*dominant area of talent*" and suggest that it helps the individual understand what enables one to "*do certain things very well* (Clifton & Anderson, 2002, 25). "

According to the research, there are as many as thirty-four separate signature themes. One individual is strong in the theme of Arranger, which means she is effective at managing seemingly uncontrollable variables to achieve a certain task. Another may be stronger in Context, so he strives to understand the "*big picture*" in a particular situation. Yet another is uniquely aware of what is special and distinct about each of the individuals with whom she interacts, the strength of Individualization.

Earlier I described that having someone pick the two strongest and the two weakest intelligences yielded seventy different possibilities within individuals. While I think that is an impressive statistic, it pales in comparison to signature themes. Clifton and Anderson ask their readers to complete a web-based inventory providing their top five signature themes. If we calculate the different ways that five themes can be selected from among the thirty-four possible themes, we find that there are 278,256 unique combinations!

Clifton and Anderson speak to how this changes the nature of the community:

> Within large or small groups, entire organizations, or even couples, two things often happen when people become aware of each other's talents. First, there is increased understanding of each other. Second, people gain greater respect for each other. Can you imagine what it would be like to live in a world where everyone understood and respected each other? Phoniness, façades, and pretense would become things of the past. Authenticity would become the new norm. And, of course, with more authenticity would

> come greater interpersonal closeness and cooperation. This would
> be a tremendous benefit of a strengths revolution! (2002, p. 280)

The norm of authenticity is an important step in the building of community. To behave with authenticity means to act in ways consistent with your uniqueness. It's opposite is to behave as you think others expect even though you suffer personal loss due to the pretense.

Let's add another layer of complexity to our roommates. For the sake of argument, I've put them both on the college's volleyball team. Becky is the team's setter and also team captain. Sarah is the defensive specialist with responsibility for taking serve from the opposing team. Becky is likely to show strength in Maximizer and Individualization. She knows where each player is on the court and who is in best position for the play. Sarah is an Achiever with a strong sense of Responsibility. She enjoys the competition and doesn't want that serve to catch her by surprise.

Coach Brown knows more than the specific talents of each player. She's been able to win conference tournaments because she knows how to get her players to make the most of each other's strengths even while playing the same positions as other players. Her game strategy is designed to make the most effective arrangement against a particular opponent. Like most Tin Men, she values the ways the players build relationships on and off the court. She wants them to be responsible for each other while performing their best.

The lessons Becky and Sarah draw from playing volleyball spill over into their classwork. They are still responsible for each other and are stronger than their individual strengths. When they graduate from college and go on into their future jobs and families, they will be building on these same lessons day after day. They will continue to refine their skills and adjust to new situations.

All of the college experience is about this kind of learning. We have to take my simple two-person example and extend it to a campus of a thousand or more. It's more complicated but the same point holds. We are very different people and we need to make those differences real parts of our discussions and activities.

We saw earlier that many emerging adults are frustrated with the institutional church even while they love Jesus. They want the church to ask complex questions because the world is a complex place. If all parts of the campus serve as sources for learning, then chapel isn't a place of escape but a place where our faith commitments come alongside the rest of life. It is a place where it's safe to disagree and to recognize that others don't think quite like I do. Chapel is a place for learning, even while it is a place for community worship.

Working through difference requires that we learn how to disagree civilly. This is a skill sorely needed in modern society. One of the byproducts of modern broadcasting and the Internet is that it becomes easy to focus on those who agree with us while demonizing those who differ. We talk in echo chambers, using dismissive tones to talk about those who are listening to other echo chambers.

This is not a model of Christian higher education. A Christian university isn't about who catches their opponent in a "gotcha moment". It's an environment based on learning. We must hear the other. We must take seriously her experiences, strengths, and ways of thinking.

It's not enough to "agree to disagree." This trite phrase is actually a roadblock to learning (it's code for pseudocommunity). If we don't engage the ideas, we don't engage the other person. That's true if the other is a roommate, teammate, coach, classmate or faculty member.

In fact, we're really characters in each other's story. We must play out those characters with authenticity and honesty. The learning of the individual depends upon it. The Good Witch of the North tells Dorothy that all she has to do is "Follow the Yellow Brick Road" in order to ask the Wizard to help her get back to Kansas. But Glinda isn't quite right. Dorothy needed the Scarecrow, the Tin Man, and the Cowardly Lion to navigate her journey. Each of them brought their unique strengths and talents to bear on their trek. Collectively, they learned great lessons about themselves. That's why they didn't need a man pretending to be a great and powerful Wizard to solve their problems for them. Every step along the Yellow Brick Road was really about learning to be who they were called to be. So it is with all of us.

9

Finding Your Own Path

Let's return to Lauren, the home-schooled student who discovered a fascination with Conrad's *Heart of Darkness*. As the first semester draws to a close, she schedules an appointment with Dr. Baldridge, her literature professor, to discuss the possibility of majoring in English. She knows she would have to read and write a lot, but she's unsure about all the other classes she is supposed to take: classes in theology or biology or fitness. She also wants to make sure that she has time during her college years to maintain her interest in student government since she was just elected to freshman council. She is passionate about her involvement in a campus group dedicated to stopping human trafficking and hopes to do volunteer work over the summer with an anti-trafficking organization.

In this chapter, we'll build on ideas from earlier chapters to see how a student like Lauren (and you) might navigate the pathways from the beginning of the college years to commencement. While we've already considered that there are organizational dynamics to university life (credits, prerequisites, mandated classes), we can use the pro-active approach to learning from the previous chapter to set the stage for successful travel down the path of higher education. Lauren will take forty-one classes designed to help her find her way (just like Larry). There are added challenges stemming from the wide range of choices available, but a proper orientation can help make that manageable.

Specifically, we'll look at three broad issues: the meaning of liberal arts education, the selection of the major, and participation in co-curricular activities. The secrets to make it all work are the things we've seen before: attention to personal story, engagement with the community, search for balance, and the discernment of the Holy Spirit. Attention to these four concerns will significantly improve your satisfaction while in school, enhance the meaning you can draw from your experiences, substantially increase your chances of sticking with it, and help you immeasurably beyond your college years.

The General Education Requirements

Dr. Baldridge tells Lauren that their university is committed to *liberal arts within a Christian context*. This seems like a nice phrase, but what does it really mean? Is it about a bunch of required classes, called general education courses, which all students must take in order to graduate? Is it about critical thinking and the examination of evidence when making arguments? And what about the Christian part? Does that mean to find scriptural foundations for chemistry class or are we trying to make everyone amateur theologians?

Given my many years of experience in Christian higher education, I'm sad to say that far too often the answer to these questions is "all of the above." This is a result of the institutional structures we explored in the chapter on why people go to college. Decisions about what's required for all students get made after years of planning and hours of meetings. Nobody wants to go back in and re-examine what we were thinking when we put the requirements together and whether they still work in the same way (especially given the realities that emerging adults are confronting!).

We don't reflect often enough on what we think is important for students to know. One of my former colleagues served on the "general education committee" of his school and realized that the structure of required classes was almost identical to what he'd had to take as a college student nearly three decades years earlier!

Let's quickly look at some of the components that you might find in your school's graduation requirements before turning to what you and Lauren ought to do about them. To begin with, many Christian liberal arts institutions may have a set of courses that are connected to the school's identity. Because the university wants to put their "stamp" on graduates, it makes sure that all students are exposed to the same ideas.

In a classic study of higher education in America (mentioned in chapter 2), Ernest Boyer makes it clear that a common curriculum of general education provides the possibility that the distinctive features of a college are imbedded in its students. Boyer refers to this as the "*integrated core*":

> By the integrated core, we mean a program of general education that introduces students not only to essential knowledge, but also to connections across the disciplines, and, in the end, to the application of knowledge to life beyond the campus. The integrated core concerns itself with the universal experiences that are common to all people, with those shared activities without which human relationships are diminished and the quality of life reduced. (1987, p. 91)

These courses are significant because they are the basis for shared experience among all students at the school, regardless of major or year. The core readings may be the same for all students because they highlight particular values.

Some schools include a senior thesis or independent project as part of the integrated core. This is an interesting twist because it allows you to pursue individual interests, but everybody does it together. You can meet an alumna at homecoming and find her talking about the importance of that one book. Another might want to ask about your senior paper and how you're preparing. The integrated core gives a common experience regardless of when you go to school.

In addition to the integrated core, nearly all Christian universities have additional courses in the Bible and theology. The Bible courses are designed to give an overview of scriptures from an academic standpoint that can enable students to speak with depth about biblical themes. The theology classes explore significant ideas of how we think about God and faith so that students are exposed to some of the big questions that have faced the Christian church over the past two millennia. These courses are important because, as we have seen, students come from a wide variety of backgrounds when it comes to religious upbringing. Some have fairly limited exposure to biblical themes (even if they know some favorite scripture passages). Others are surprised to find that the questions they've been asking themselves are questions Christians have dealt with for centuries.

There are still others who come from churches that spent much time in Bible studies and apologetics. The challenge for these students may be to find that there are alternative yet legitimate ways of thinking about faith and they need to make space for those.[1] They will also need to manage the moments of chaos that result when this vast array of students comes together around the study of scripture and doctrine.

---

1. We spent considerable time examining these differences in chapter 7.

Courses designed to develop skills that lead to college success form a third piece of general education. This category includes classes like freshman composition, argumentation, math or statistics, speech, and perhaps computer[2] courses. In most institutions, there are very specific classes you are asked to take and pass successfully. The assumption is that you will keep using the skills developed in these classes in all other classes in college and in the world beyond graduation.

A fourth set of classes comprises what are called "distributive requirements." These courses are most closely associated with the liberal arts goals of exposing students to the vast array of perspectives within the college. Regardless of your area of specialization, it's good to know a bit about the contributions other perspectives can bring.

The distributive requirements typically instruct you to "pick one course from the following list" within a specific category. It's good to be exposed to the natural sciences, literature, foreign languages, social sciences, the fine arts, and fitness/nutrition. You might not pursue these areas on your own but may find that they enrich your life in important ways. Not in every class perhaps, but you can often make some surprising connections. That history of drama class can spark a lifelong interest in going to plays. The biology class may help you understand climate change debates.

Many schools also have experiential requirements. You'll find these in service learning opportunities and study abroad excursions. Sometimes these expectations are built into particular classes (i.e., volunteer fifteen hours at the homeless shelter). Others may involve short-term overseas trips designed to expose you to non-American lifestyles.

Given this array of classes Lauren is supposed to take, it's not surprising that she's confused. If you don't find this array of options somewhat overwhelming, you're not being honest with yourself. So what is Lauren to do?

It was good that she sat down with her professor to work through the choices. It's daunting (and based on my college experience, dangerous) to try to navigate all by yourself. If you only see a bingo-sheet of requirements and try to fill them in on your own, you may make errors that not only inhibit your enjoyment, but can also cost you real money! There's nothing scarier than a note from the registrar's office coming during the second

---

2. These may become less necessary as the technological sophistication of incoming students continues to build.

semester of your senior year saying that you're missing one required class and will need to return in the fall.

Dr. Baldridge is a scarecrow that lives for medieval English. It's not her fault. As we saw in the Wizard of Oz chapter, she's committed herself to years of study in this particular area. Truth be told, she may not know a lot about the natural sciences and may find chemistry particularly scary.

This uncertainty is what prompts too many faculty members to take the bingo-sheet approach to general education. You hear this in comments like, "let's get this out of the way this semester." It is vitally important that Lauren and Dr. Baldridge avoid this tendency. You don't want to take a particular requirement just because you need three more hours to make full time or because there's an early afternoon section available. You don't want to just pick the first thing recommended in the catalog and thereby fulfill the requirement.

I can offer some advice on how to make the most of these general requirements. Don't think of them as a set of individual choices you have to make but a series of steps toward a goal. Here's an example: A colleague of mine instructs the jazz band at his college. I once asked him how he put a music program together. He told me that he determined the piece he wanted to close with and then decided on the opening. Everything else fell together along the way.

That makes me think of a related example. Some of you may have experience leading worship in church or at camp. You don't just pick the song that "fits" but you think about what the overall message is. The songs sung at the beginning of the service are coordinated with the central theme of the message and the closing song underscores the takeaway point.

One more illustration comes from a colleague who teaches writing. He tells his classes about the difference between looking at a map and going on a tour. When you look at a map, you have all the information necessary about distances between places but don't really know what you're seeing. On a tour, you have a guide who has already spent time in the area, can show you why these paths are better than those, and can introduce you to some interesting sights along the way. Your smartphone may be able to get you from one point to another but without a story to inform the route, the trip can be lifeless. You *look* at a map but you go on a tour. The tour is an active and participatory process.

These examples begin to show how we can approach the host of choices present in those forty-one classes between the start and finish of college.

Rather than seeing the big bingo-sheet as something to be managed, we can see the required courses as means to a larger end. Seeing them as means reflects the larger reality that these everyday experiences may be Means of Grace through which you draw closer to God and develop a fuller sense of yourself.

Turning the bingo-sheet into a meaningful guide to pursuing your goals requires a shift in mentality similar to what we saw in the last chapter. It requires an active, reflective orientation toward your coursework. Ken Bain, who discussed Stephen Colbert's journey in an earlier chapter, addressed these concerns in an earlier book of his. This book, *What the Best College Teachers Do*, focuses on excellent teachers (Bain, 2004), but it has some interesting ideas about student learning.

Bain's teachers saw that good students have become *"deep learners"* rather than giving into the temptation to be *"bulimic learners."* Deep Learners plan tasks to be accomplished that serve as markers toward specified goals, even if it detracts from true learning. Bulimic Learners do exactly what it sounds like: binging and purging. They put all that stuff into their heads prior to an exam or assignment, cross it off their to-do list, and then vacate their craniums to make room for the next exam or assignment. It's just as unhealthy as the eating disorder it's named for.

Too many students (and their faculty) approach the array of required classes as a set of individual meals to be consumed rather than a long-term commitment to a healthy diet. Once a particular course is over it can be filed away, the books resold, the mind emptied, and then you are ready for the next semester. This is the primary reason that the so-called "skills classes" don't transfer to life practices. Once the last assignment for freshmen composition is over, bulimic studiers clear their brains and begin the next class.

Instead, if you learn to use your required classes toward a larger end, the whole liberal arts experience begins to take shape. You take information from your history class to understand what's currently going on in the Middle East. You find ways of revisiting the play you read for your Shakespeare course in the junior level management course. You use material from your psychology class to think about how to interact with that one cousin at family gatherings. Your fitness class helps you assist your brother in recovering from his sports injury.

The deep learning approach also builds the community we examined in chapter 6. By taking a wide variety of classes, you gain invaluable insights into the other members of the community. When I first met my wife, she was a graduate student in mathematics and geology. I was still completing my undergraduate degree. I decided to take geology as an elective course just so I could understand the tremendous hold it had on her. Even though I only passed with a C, I achieved the goal of understanding her world (and her) a little better. Now, when our vacations inevitably involve geologic sites, I experience the trip through her eyes.

Let's go back, for a moment, to Becky and Sarah. If Becky is a Biology major and Sarah is an English major, they need the core curriculum to see through each other's eyes. If community is formed through negotiating common understandings, one must be able to grasp how the other thinks. This can happen more readily as Becky learns the power of *Moby Dick* and Sarah comes to understand the intricacies of cell behavior. The courses become windows into those around them.

The classes that make up the core experience for students are not something to be "gotten out of the way." Too often these courses are seen as rites of passage that everyone has to go through because it's just part of the game. However, the required general education coursework provides a unique opportunity for you to understand yourself in new ways, to deeply connect with others, and to create the possibility for a significant sense of community.

Choosing the Major

Now that Lauren and Dr. Baldridge have a new understanding of graduation requirements, it's time to talk about her interest in majoring in English. If the core curriculum provides the means for understanding others in the community, the major provides the opportunity for fine-tuning one's gifts and calling. Notice that I am not suggesting that the role of the major is simply to find a job. The job is a critical byproduct of the pursuit of the major but not the goal of the major itself.

Most students come to college with a generic sense of what they plan to do with their lives following college. When you came to orientation, the first questions you asked everyone were, "Where are you from?" and "What's your major?" You've got a firm answer to the first, but might be much more tentative about the second.[3]

---

3. We put way too much pressure on students to firm up these choices too early. My son had an eighth grade assignment on what one would do with a given major, complete

If one interviews incoming college students, that general sense of direction is expressed as "exploring God's world," "doing something in business," "just helping people," "developing my music," "serving the church," or "living in a foreign country." Our concern with the academic major unfortunately blinds people to these deep-seated longings. Being a biology major, a business major, a social work major, a music composition major, a religion major, or a Spanish major is nothing more than shorthand for a series of common courses identified by an academic department as providing the essential body of knowledge for the subject in question.

But the list of courses that must be completed before graduation is not the same thing as the general sense of direction the student brings in. While all biology majors will be completing the same set of classes as Becky and are therefore interacting with the same information, each one of them is pursuing a slightly different sense of why that information is relevant and they will each connect with the course material in unique ways.

There is a tendency to substitute the accumulation of specific course credits for the pursuit of the student's future. *The timeline for the major is not the four years of college but the forty years after graduation.* How are these classes paving the way for your future activities?

There is much concern in the media about students changing majors during the college career. If the major is only about the accumulation of the specific courses, then a change of major from education to music (or vice versa) means that courses were "wasted" because they are no longer relevant to the check sheet of the new major. The religion major that becomes a psychology or sociology major may be seen as abandoning an area of study for another and therefore starting from scratch. Instead, the religion major is pursuing his path in ways he feels God is leading. Nothing is "lost" in the process even when pursuing a more "secular" major.

There is another sense in which there is something much deeper going on within the academic major. Lurking behind and beneath the general sense of direction is often a "Dream". This Dream is a tangible idea of what the student hopes to be doing at some point in the future. It is a very personal story[4] and may even be embarrassing to share with anyone. But the

---

with family budget. Nobody knows enough to make life choices of this magnitude at thirteen. Doing so at eighteen is scary enough.

4. This is why I've often argued that it would be wonderful for all students to craft an individualized major and explain why they planned on taking the classes they selected.

Dream is significant precisely because it is the end point of the general sense of direction. Parker Palmer describes the idea of The Dream as follows:

> Discovering vocation does not mean scrambling toward some prize just beyond my reach but accepting the treasure of true self I already possess. Vocation does not come from a voice *out there* calling me to be something I am not. It comes from a voice *in here* calling me to be the person I was born to be, to fulfill the original selfhood given me at birth by God. (Palmer, 2000, p. 10, emphasis in original)

Here's an example of a Dream. A student had come to meet with me to discuss majoring in social justice (one of the tracks within sociology). I asked him what he wanted to do. His response was that of all college students: "*I don't know.*" I asked him what he imagined doing with his degree after graduation and he said, "*I don't know.*" I asked him if he ever had a Dream of what he'd like to do ten years after graduation and he said, "*I don't know.*" I suggested that there might, at some point, have been an idea so outrageous that he wouldn't share it with his parents, pastor, or teachers.

I was ready for another "*I don't know.*" I was amazed when he instead responded, "*Well, you know I live in the upper peninsula of Michigan and I've always liked the outdoors, especially horses. I've thought it would be wonderful to buy some land and establish a ranch with horses. I'd have juvenile delinquents from Detroit who have never been out of the city come out to my place and experience the horses and the community for a week at a time. I'd have a youth minister on the staff because I'm not that good at that. We'd have programs on personal responsibility and tutoring and maybe keep these kids out of future trouble.*" I told him for not knowing what he wanted to do, that was pretty amazing.

This story would be even more amazing if I could tell you that seventeen years later he was living on a ranch in Michigan caring for juvenile delinquents from Detroit. That's how it would work in the movies. The truth is that I've lost track of him and don't know where he is. But reality doesn't change the power of the Dream. It doesn't matter if he's working on the ranch or serving as a police officer or doing something else God called him to.

The English major, then, is nothing more than a tool that Lauren will use to explore her unfolding future. It is a means to a greater end. It is a more narrow area of focus because few of us can be renaissance people who are able to find our direction in the breadth of the college curriculum (although those I have known are truly amazing people). But it must always remain in service of the Dream and the general direction.

In this light, a student who changes from a religion major to a psychology major so as to better help the people in a yet-to-come congregation is simply finding the unique path from the present to the anticipated future. The major is about exposure to the key elements of the field that are selectively applied to the student's future experiences. As we saw with the curriculum as a whole, when the time horizon shifts from the four years of college to the student's life, the role of the major becomes starkly clear. It is an important road map for the journey but it is never the destination.

One more thing I want to share about the choice of academic direction. I often have students asking me about the value of squeezing in another minor or what will happen to their prospects if they don't stay with the minor they had planned on. Minors are valuable and departments create them to aid someone who wants a little specialization. It's better in a rapidly changing world to have a secondary area than to be overly focused on only one thing. But the minor itself is just a name we give to a bunch of classes.

At the same time, the pursuit of the Dream means that you can talk intelligently about how you put your classes together. Becky can explain to a prospective employer that she took a number of Spanish courses alongside her biology major because she has a passion to work with poor families in the Southwest. That testimony is going to carry far more weight than a designation on her diploma or transcript (which the employer is unlikely to look at anyway).

All of these decisions about courses provide you with a unique approach to your education. You may have the same major as someone else, but it's your story. There may be students taking the same general education classes, but you're taking away perspectives that inform your own deep learning.

Selecting Extra-Curricular Activities

We saw in chapter 2 that one of the advantages of coming to a Christian university is its smaller size, especially when contrasted with the state school and its tens of thousands of students. The smaller size means that you can form lasting relationships with classmates, get involved in activities, and try out lots of opportunities. In fact, it's possible to dabble in lots of different things in ways that are hard to achieve at a larger institution.

For example, it's very difficult to go to an audition for a drama production at the big school: slots are generally designated for people in the theater program. "Walking on" as an athlete works in the movies but is much more rare in real life.

On the other hand, a smaller liberal arts institution provides greater opportunity to be in student ministry, sing in the choir, run track, join the college republicans, etc. As we saw, all of these activities can become valuable avenues for learning and growth. But the very range of those opportunities can present a real challenge for even the most motivated student.

I wrote earlier about Howard Gardner's work on multiple intelligences. Some people "think" spatially, others physically, others linguistically, still others in interaction with others, and more. This is very relevant here. What is the motivation for someone to play soccer in college? If Gardner is correct, that suggests that someone plays soccer because it's a natural expression of his very being. While he knows that he will never make the World Cup, he continues to play because it's how he restores himself.

That's not true for everyone. Some students got involved in soccer when they were four years old and have been playing ever since. They continue because they've invested all that time and the family seems to like their participation. If soccer is not a natural part of life, continuation in soccer may not be fulfilling (and could even be damaging).

Over the years, I have seen many students wrestle with the demands of their special skill (whether athletics, music, or drama) in the college environment. There are many reasons for this.

First, there is more of an even talent level in college than there was in the past. A basketball player might have been successful simply by being the tallest guy on the high school team. Playing against smaller players meant that he could star without pushing himself. Once he gets to college, he finds out that his teammates (as well as those for other colleges) are just as good as the best players he ever faced in high school, maybe better. Now what seemed like a fun after-school activity begins to become real work. He must develop his game, learn new strategies, spend hours in the weight room, and continually prove himself against others. The coach will push and prod, which feels awkward after the relationship building of the recruiting process. The student will be tempted to spend much of his free time with the basketball team.

If basketball is part of his very way of being, he'll be thrilled with these new demands. He'll be learning new things, improving his skills, and become more connected to his innate talents than ever before. If it's not part of his being, this will feel like pain and create dissatisfaction. He may even question whether this college is where he's supposed to be.

We could tell the exact same story if you are a student in drama productions, the drummer for the worship band, the candidate for freshman class president, or the bible study leader. There will be people at least as talented, experienced, and motivated as you. What passed for acceptable performance before will be harder to achieve. You won't be appreciated nearly as much as you are used to. If developing these talents is in your bones, you'll adjust. If it's simply something you like or gives you visibility, it will be a struggle.

So one challenge of navigating extra-curricular activities is maintaining connection to identity. But, there remains the issue of how such activities compete with your academic life.

Ernest Pascarella is one of the leading specialists on how students succeed in college (known as persistence). He and some colleagues conducted a highly complex statistical study of learning over the freshman year[5] for college athletes at a variety of universities (Pascarella, Bohr, Nora, & Terenzini, 1995). Their statistical methods allowed them to examine any impact of athletic participation independent of the students' background before college. They found by the end of the freshman year that athletes showed lower scores on reading comprehension than non-athletes.

Why would this be the case? They suggest two factors might be in play. First, they recognize that athletic participation (particularly in the big sports like basketball, football, and baseball) require significant time commitments that can interfere with academic performance even while teaching discipline. Second, they suggest that some athletic teams create a somewhat insulated culture that values the athletic group over all other activities. The two factors are related. The more time you spend with a group, the more important they become. Team sports depend upon a high level of trust and bonding.

I'm sure Ernest Pascarella loves his Hawkeyes as much as the next University of Iowa professor. His analysis isn't a critique of athletics. It's an accurate reflection of the challenges of extra-curricular engagement.

It would be easy to see the same combination of high time commitments and in-group orientation in student government, ministry groups,

---

5. This uses different measures but is similar in style to the *Academically Adrift* analysis in the previous chapter.

or drama. Each is an important activity and requires a significant investment of time and emotional energy. Sometimes those activities come at particular bad times. For example, major drama productions often fall around homecoming, which also happens to be close to midterms. At exactly the point where things get busier in the classroom, the drama folks are spending five to six hours an evening in dress rehearsals.

Two things help you navigate these extracurricular issues. The first is to find a sense of balance that allows you to pursue competing activities. The second is to pay attention to your calendar and emotional energy. This balance requires constant vigilance. It's not really about giving all things equal time, but about understanding the competing demands on your time. It's hard, but you really don't get to choose between good options. You wind up going to practice *and* keeping up with your reading.

I once had a conversation with a girl involved in student government. She told me that she really wanted to get everything possible out of the relationship side of college life, so was willing to settle for Bs in all her classes. I was saddened because she failed to work at balance. She just sacrificed part of the college experience for another part.

Balance will become very difficult to maintain if you're one of those students who dabbles in a little bit of everything. If you do debate *and* choir *and* government *and* track *and* coursework, something will give. Most likely it will start with cutting back on sleep and progress into actual physical illness.

Back in chapter 2 we looked at the work of UCLA's Higher Education Research Institute and their annual freshman survey. In addition to exploring motivations for college choice, HERI collects data on student emotional well-being. This data has been an ongoing discussion topic for college administrators. Just over half of college freshman report being in the highest levels of emotional health. Nearly three in ten report feeling "overwhelmed" during their senior year in high school (Pryor et al., 2011).

This experience of stress or anxiety is a natural part of the college transition. If you look back at the ground we've covered in this chapter, you should feel stressed! It's a lot to manage: required classes, selecting the major, participating in co-curricular activities. As much as you want to "have it all," it really can't be done. There isn't enough time in the day. Even if you try the occasional all-nighter, it won't relieve the stress.

Of course, some students experience stress from external factors as well. There may be health issues, an impending parental divorce, financial struggles, or a bad relationship back home.

How, then, do you manage the inevitable stress you feel? Here are several strategies to keep in mind. First, keep your routine. Sure, there are a lot of reasons why you don't go to bed as early when you live in a residence hall as you did when you lived at home. But patterns are helpful. Sleep about the same number of hours each night and organize your homework and social life around that. Learn to take naps (but not during class!).

Second, recognize that there are times when stress levels will be unusually high. Plan for those. If there's a paper due during the week of the drama production, you better start it ten days early. If you have a major presentation coming up in your political science class, don't be the leader for the Bible study that week.

Third, don't sweat the choices you have to make. That may seem to contradict my earlier points but you need to remember that life is full of choices. Over the years, I've often had students come to me with a story like this: "*My roommate just went through a major breakup and I felt she needed me. I stayed up talking and praying with her and I didn't get to study for your exam.*" The student then wants to get an excuse[6] for a later test or a retake. But pushing back the exam will only interfere with the rest of the semester's work in my class and others. Far better that my student recognize that she made a choice of what to do with her time (probably the right one) and will wind up with a lower grade on this particular test as a result. And then move on.

Fourth, know who you are. This will help you sort the things that are central from the things that are nice but not essential. Part of this also involves knowing your physical warning signs. Over the years, I've learned that when I'm highly stressed I carry the stress in my shoulders and start minimizing interaction with others (a telltale sign for high interpersonal intelligence). When I become aware of my indicators, I know I have to take a break. I'll be far more productive afterward, much more than if I pushed through my workload while distracted by the stress.

Finally, listen for the voice of the Holy Spirit. Those gentle nudges we call conscience don't occur just when you're tempted to do bad things. They happen all along the way. You may be travelling this complicated road of

---

6. Forgive a professor's nagging that if she'd started studying for the exam earlier than the night before the test the conflict would be lessened.

courses, activities, and just plain life but you never do so alone. The Spirit is faithful, sometimes speaking through your roommate, sometimes through a text from your mom, sometimes through chapel, and sometimes even through your sociology professor.

At the close of the *Wizard of Oz*, Dorothy found out that she could be comfortable at home. What I pray for you is that you'll find "home" wherever you find yourself along the road. It's not a final place but a sense of contentment in the midst of transition.

10

Practicing the Kingdom

Scott Daniels is a pastor in Pasadena, CA and dean of the school of theology at Azusa Pacific University. He recently spent a full year preaching from the Gospel of Mark. He began every one of those sermons with the same phrase: *"There are many sermons in the Gospel of Mark but only one message: The Kingdom of God is at hand!"*

The entire book we've been heading to this point. The Christian University of which you are a part is both an outpost and an exemplar of the Kingdom of God itself. It is an outpost because it operates on Kingdom principles. It is an exemplar because it provides models for engaging the broader culture. In this final chapter, I'll explain what scholars mean by the Kingdom and show how the themes we've explored connect to illustrate what Christian higher education looks like in a postmodern age.

Here's one final Wizard of Oz reference. When Dorothy and friends *"follow the yellow brick road,"* they finally end up at the Emerald City. What is this destination like? It's a grand place, with green horses, and pretty people and pomp and ceremony. Dorothy and friends get fixed up[1] so that they can have their meeting with the Great and Powerful Wizard of Oz. But it proves to be a lot of illusion. People really aren't that happy, the horse is dyed, and the Wizard is a fraud. The end of their long journey turns out to be a pseudocommunity that doesn't provide them with safety or answers.

This is what a credential-based college education offers. Yes, you have the diploma and can call yourself a graduate. But then what? What life lessons do you take with you? What are the mechanisms you'll use to navigate uncertain waters?

1. There are some very interesting similarities to *The Hunger Games.*

The Christian university is far more than a means to a degree. We aren't simply providing a standard university education and adding in required chapel, prayer before class, or talk about Christian implications of astronomy. What we are doing is fundamentally different: *We are embodying the Kingdom of God.*

The Kingdom of God

Let me unpack this Kingdom of God imagery before we move on by focusing on three biblical scholars. There are many others, but looking at N. T. Wright, Scot McKnight, and Walter Brueggemann will begin to paint a picture of the Kingdom in our midst.

N. T. Wright, has also written extensively on this topic. In his recent book *How God Became King* (Wright, 2012), he explores how we've promoted slightly distorted understandings of God's work in Christ. When we get those understandings appropriately aligned, we see that God was working to restore Creation all along. This understanding of God's work in our midst changes the ways we engage the world around us. Here is how he put it in a slightly earlier work (Wright, 2010):

> Jesus came, in fact, to launch God's new creation, and with it a new way of being human, a way which picked up the glimpses of "right behavior" afforded by ancient Judaism and paganism and transcending both on quite a new foundation. And with that, he launched also a project for rehumanizing human beings, a project in which they would find their hearts cleansed and softened, find themselves turned upside down and inside out, and discover a new language to learn and every incentive to learn it. God's kingdom was bursting into the present world, offering a "goal" the like of which Aristotle had never imagined. Human beings were called at last to discover what they had been made for, what Israel had been created for. (p. 133)

Scot McKnight is a New Testament scholar at Northern Seminary near Chicago. His book, *The King Jesus Gospel* (McKnight, 2011), argues that our heavy focus on Jesus' death on the cross (called soteriology—the understanding of salvation) keeps us from understanding the birth of the Kingdom (which is the full Good News). He's not arguing against the need for individual salvation but he is suggesting that bigger things are going on. God is completing his original plan for Creation through the death and resurrection of Jesus and the leading of the church by the Spirit.

We can pick up similar teaching in the work of Old Testament scholar Walter Brueggemann. He artfully considers the lessons learned by the Israelites in slavery in Egypt, in exile in Babylon, and in the teachings of the prophet Isaiah. They turn out, not surprisingly, to echo the themes of the New Testament scholars above. Here is his concluding passage from *Journey to the Common Good*:

> Thus I intend that these chapters might recruit and summon religious communities that derive from biblical faith and so might aid in the recovery of nerve about truth telling and hope telling. Beyond the public vocation of the religious communities funded by biblical imagination, moreover, it is my hope that they may invite us, yet again, to be dazzled by the compelling passion of the God who indwells the text. In, with, and under all of our political and theological claims, there is this holy will, purpose, and presence that does not quit. It is holiness marked by a severe fidelity. (Bruggemann, 2010, pp. 121–22)

Everything discussed in the book has been based on the assumption that something special is happening at your Christian university. You have left home, with its comfort and security (at least for most), and you have ventured forth into a new world. But that world isn't just the next step after your high school experience—it's the petri dish where you'll practice living as a citizen of the Kingdom of God.

There are those who suggest that the Kingdom of God cannot be experienced until the life to come. In his best-selling book, *The Purpose Driven Life* (2002), Saddleback Church pastor Rick Warren describes our daily behavior as "practice" for our home in heaven. Our benchmark should be to model the kinds of devotion to God that will be needed in a worship-filled eternity.

While I understand Warren's passion, it is important to recognize that when we put the Kingdom of God into practice it makes a difference in our lives today. Describing the specific nature of that difference has occasionally been a point of challenge.

Over a decade ago, I heard evangelical speaker (and sociologist), Tony Campolo, claim that graduates of our institutions should find it hard to work in the secular environment because their sense of ethics was so deeply ingrained. In fact, they should expect to be fired for their principled stands.

This argument created great distress among many Christian university business faculty. They argued that their students had spent a lot of time and effort on ethics and personal responsibility. They would be able to freely confront unethical employees and are capable of being solid Christian leaders.

Of course, both arguments have some merit. Campolo was saying that the Christian university must instill countercultural values in its graduates. The business faculty were assuring themselves that they had covered those materials in lectures and course assignments.

Both would agree that the ethos of the Christian university would be put into play immediately upon graduation and entry into "the world." Students would know how to firmly state their values and faithfully hold their positions, even if they risked losing a job as a result.

But based on the arguments I have been advancing, the viewpoints of Warren, Campolo, and the business faculty still remain limited. The Kingdom imagery does apply to the here and now, but it is not because students have learned the "right" answers to ethical dilemmas. It's not simply a matter of knowing principles. It's not about having the "Christian" answers to every dilemma.

The Kingdom of God is the central theme of the Christian university. It is our way of being. We aren't simply preparing for the Kingdom; we are experiencing it on a daily basis. In so doing, we're helping establish it in the broader society.

On one level, it's easy to see this in operation. Today's Christian university students are passionate about caring for the victimized. You take very seriously the instruction in Micah 6:8, "*What does the Lord require of you but to do justice, to love kindness, and to walk humbly with your God?*"

You are involved in all kinds of groups advancing justice. Just take a quick survey of Facebook pages and even t-shirt logos. You can quickly see concerns about Invisible Children, Aids orphans, the unborn, and sex trafficking victims.

Look at where students spend the free time of spring break, summers, or even weekends. Students like you can be found cleaning up areas ravaged by natural disasters, ministering to the homeless, caring for the elderly, or serving a mission in Thailand.

Why do you do this? Because you see it as something you can change. In your own little way, you are contributing to the visibility of the Kingdom of God.

I assigned the book *Kisses From Katie* (Davis, 2011) to one of my classes. While it's not a story of a college student, it's close. Katie Davis left her evangelical home in the Nashville area to teach in Uganda. Along the way she winds up adopting over a dozen children while still a single woman in her early twenties. It's a compelling story. To be honest, I thought I'd use it as a case study of why students needed to be prepared for the challenges of world-saving; Katie's blind faith and endless enthusiasm kind of scared me a bit. But my students loved Katie. They recognized that there were challenges and hard times, but they admired her commitment to Jesus and her willingness to make a difference in the world around her.

While there are exceptions, students today don't believe the world is fated to be on a downward spiral to apocalypse. They believe they can build a better Kingdom; not in their own strength of wisdom but by attending to Micah 6:8.

In the midst of this desire to build a better world, I offer a few suggestions. First, don't expect everyone else to share your passions. The person in the next dorm room may be just as passionate about a different issue. Another student may have had a specific experience that causes him to see the problem very differently.[2] Second, don't get overly optimistic in your goals. I recently saw a poster announcing a fundraiser to "end human slavery." I appreciate the goal, but slowing the growth of human slavery is a big enough task. There are "powers and principalities" in operation on some of these issues and change may take generations. Third, don't let the enormity of the issues overwhelm you. I teach a social problems class in a three-week term. We cover fifteen major problems in fifteen days. I wind up demoralized and I'm familiar with the material! Finally, make a commitment that you'll make social engagement a way of life and not a momentary thing. There is a tendency to engage when surrounded by like-minded college people. It's harder to maintain over the long haul. Don't let the normalcy of daily life numb you to big justice issues you care about now. Together, over time, we can do justice, love kindness, and walk humbly as a way of life that changes the world.

The Kingdom and the College

As proud as I am of your passion for the world, the Kingdom of God isn't just something "out there." Sometimes, "one of the least of these" (Matthew

---

2. For example, while you may be absolutely passionate about protecting unborn children, another student whose sister got pregnant at a very young age may see the situation as more complex.

25) is sitting in class right next to you. Throughout this book, the educational goal has been to create the space where all students will become their most vibrant selves for the good of all.

How does the idea of God's Kingdom connect to education? A quick review of some favored passages from the synoptic Gospels shows Jesus spending a lot of time trying to give his hearers a glimpse of the Kingdom. There are stories of Jesus connecting with people where they are (Zacchaeus, the Woman caught in Adultery, the Woman at the Well, the Woman with the Alabaster Jar). There are stories of breaking down past expectations (the Good Samaritan, Healing on the Sabbath). There are many parables of new approaches to justice (the parable of the debtor, the parable of the workers in the field, the parable of the talents).

I want to tread carefully here so that I'm not misunderstood. But it strikes me that none of Jesus' descriptions or examples of the Kingdom involved stuff you believe. Not a case where he says, "*The Kingdom of God is like a bunch of people who got together and discussed the rightness of their answers compared to those in the broader society.*" He does speak to attitudes in the Sermon on the Mount (teachings on anger, lust, worry). He does say that as we think, so we are. But that's not about *what* we think.

Biblical knowledge, understandings of theology, and awareness of the major questions in church history are important. They tell us about the tradition of the church (one of the key components of Wesley's approach to theology). But their value comes especially in how it shapes our acting. *To put it the other way around, what we say we know is unimportant if it doesn't impact how we live.*

Most of what we've looked at in this book has been about how we live. It begins in recognizing that we each have a story. That story is more than the events of your upbringing, happy or sad memories, family characteristics, triumphs and failures. It is both a part of your identity and an expectation of where you are headed.

The elements of your story shape who you are. You see the world in a particular way because of your story. Just like in a novel, the past elements present a likely path your life may follow in the future. Here's the thing. When we become active characters in each other's story, the path into the future changes. We find new ways to become more than we ever thought possible.

The Christian university that models the Kingdom of God celebrates stories: both those from the past and those in the making. It means that we are ultimately responsible for how each other's stories turn out. As Scott Peck said, we work toward community. And as Dietrich Bonheoffer said, that community is a gift of God's grace.

This is why it's so important for Michael to understand Brandon's position in social problems class and for them to work through their differences to mutual benefit. It's why Becky and Sarah work to understand their volleyball teammates and seek to make Coach Brown a more compassionate mentor.

One of the sad realities of higher education is that not everybody who begins college finishes. Actually, depending on the school, twenty to forty percent of the freshmen won't return the following year. Some of that is due to external factors; family crisis, health issues, finances.

Much of it is simple neglect. It comes about because the student lost a sense of balance between the various demands. It happens because, like me at eighteen, they gave up a bit. I want to encourage those of you tempted by these factors that you can resist them and keep your focus on learning, wherever you are.

But I also need to encourage the rest of us that we are part of each other's stories. We're part of the story of that one guy who seems to spend all hours playing pool in the game room. Or that girl who is always taking three-hour lunches so she can socialize in the dining commons. Or the guy in the computer lab who spends hours on Facebook with folks back home but doesn't do his schoolwork.

Most schools have some kind of early warning system that will let someone know that one of these students is in academic trouble. Faculty members are encouraged to let someone know that the pool-guy's grades have dropped off or the lunch girl has been missing classes.

These are good as far as they go, but they're relatively ineffective. That's because they take a long time for the situation to get severe enough for someone to make a report. But pool-guy's friends knew he was skipping class. Facebook-guy's roommates were sitting near him in the computer lab working on their classwork while he was chatting with friends back home. *If you're part of the story, you have an obligation to the ending.*[3] If one of these guys doesn't return to school, you are a small part of the reason. In the Kingdom of God, we don't leave things to chance. We invest ourselves in seeing that the other person's story ends well.

3. This is another lesson from 1 Corinthians 12.

We're part of the story of that faculty member whose insecurity and fear keeps him from relating to his students. We're part of the story of the dean of students that has put maintaining order above mentoring. We're part of the story of the college president who knows that the school should deal with some racial issues but is afraid of making news.

The Apostle Paul reminds us in Ephesians that we all have different roles to play:

> And He gave some as apostles, and some as prophets, and some as evangelists, and some as pastors and teachers, for the equipping of the saints for the work of service, to the building up of the body of Christ; until we all attain to the unity of the faith, and of the knowledge of the Son of God, to a mature [person], to the measure of the stature which belongs to the fullness of Christ. (Eph 4:11–13)

Notice a couple of things in Paul's language. First, all of these roles are necessary to build up the body of Christ (which is the work of the Kingdom of God). There's no indication of a hierarchy here. Second, while God's sovereignty is shown in the various roles, it doesn't mean that we don't know about the other roles. It means we all have a part to play in seeing those roles fulfilled. We have to understand how each piece works in order to play our own role.

Clearly Paul wasn't thinking about universities when he wrote the church in Ephesus. But it's consistent with our understanding of the Christian university as the Kingdom of God to imagine the verse reading, "*He gave some as Scarecrows, some as Tin Men, some as Lions, and some as Young Girls looking to get home . . .*"

If you have a class with the insecure professor who maintains such distance that learning suffers, part of your role as a student is to help the professor overcome his fear and to find himself in his calling. You do that by learning some of his story, showing interest in the topic he's invested his life in, and by doing your part to make the class an inviting and welcoming place. The one thing you don't want to do is make him irrelevant. Don't make him an obstacle to your own success or simply someone to be endured. You owe this to the professor, to his colleagues, to your classmates, and to future students. If you were just racking up credits toward graduation, this wouldn't be necessary. But you're helping form the Kingdom of God.

The situation with the dean of students is similar. She so much wants you to develop moral character that it's a temptation for her to get impatient and want her students to be more than they're capable of being. What do you do when you, or maybe a friend of yours, needs to have a difficult conversation about discipline? You affirm the path that you're on. She values growth. Admit any mistakes you made. If it's a friend in trouble, help the friend own the situation as a point of growth. Reflecting with the dean on what went wrong and what to do about it speaks directly to her heart and her calling. She's not the enemy but someone trying to follow the path before her. If college were about being a partier as the movies suggest, you can play the victim. But you are building the Kingdom of God. It calls for engagement, honesty, repentance, and growth.

The college president's role is a little different, because most of you don't have access to the president. Sure, there may be the off chance of a meal in the cafeteria but you really don't know what she does on a daily basis. Nevertheless, you're part of the racial atmosphere of your campus. You should be going out of your way to examine your attitudes and to explore those whose experiences are different than yours. Because you are helping the president to be courageous, you should avoid private or public attacks. Stay away from incendiary Facebook posts or random e-mail blasts. You have an obligation to change the situation on the ground, because you're embodying the Kingdom of God. Maybe the best way to help the president is to simply invite him to listen in as you and your friends discuss the racial climate on campus.

That's the message of Paul's body imagery we looked at in chapter 6. He speaks of how the eye and ear are each essential. If not for them, how would our senses work? It's worth repeating the close of that passage:

> But God has so composed the body, giving more abundant honor to that member which lacked, so that there may be no division in the body, but that the members may have the same care for one another. And if one member suffers, all the members suffer with it; if one member is honored, all the members rejoice with it. Now you are Christ's body, and individually members of it. (1 Corinthians 12:24–27)

The message Paul is sharing is the essential sociological notion of interdependence. We don't do things on our own. Our actions, thoughts, and attitudes are shaped by the thoughts, attitudes and actions of others.[4]

4. This is a paraphrase of the classical definition of social psychology.

Because we're concerned about the entire body, each part plays its unique role. The body isn't healthy if that's not the case. Because we value each part, no part is elevated as being more significant than any other. It's not about the parts; it's about the whole.

My performance as a college professor is interdependent with your performance as a college student. It's interdependent with how my colleagues behave, whether they are teachers or coaches. It's interdependent with how the college president goes about her job. Of course, your experience is interdependent with each of these other roles as well. It's interdependent with all the students around you. It's even interdependent with the students who went to school in the past and helped establish a campus culture.

This, then, is what it means for the Christian university to embody the Kingdom of God. It's a place where we are attending to each other's stories, our roles, our gifts, and our possibilities. It's a place where those differences are the beginning point of community and not the end-point of individual expression or accomplishment. It's a place where we celebrate all parts of "the body." It's a place where we aren't afraid of anything because the Holy Spirit is leading us individually and collectively.

This should remind us of Wesley's approach to theology. We study the Scripture and understand our Traditions. We live our lives together and use our Experiences as the sources of new learning. We use our Reason and consciences to sort out the rough patches that are inevitably part of the transitions that include us all. Through this, we affirm the presence of Jesus Christ whose Spirit is leading us to all truth.

In the community chapter, I mentioned the work of Daniel Goleman and his colleagues (Goleman et al., 2002) on how emotional intelligence leads to organizational health. When I first read the book, I exchanged e-mails with co-author Richard Boyatzis (Boyatzis, 2003) on how such health shows up in a university setting. He told me that anytime I found myself in a committee meeting where concern for the common good seemed to settle on the room instead of personal interest, we were getting close. I think he's right, as far as it goes. But the Christian University as Kingdom of God is more than that.

In his science fiction trilogy, C. S. Lewis imagines some very interesting alternatives to Creation and the Fall. Part of the stories involve interaction with what he calls Eldil; roughly what we'd think of as angels. In the opening of *Perelandra* (his book about Venus and the Fall), he has the narrator recounting his interaction with the Eldil:

> What I saw was very simply a very faint rod or pillar of light . . .
> But it had two other characteristics which are less easy to grasp.
> One was its colour . . . no efforts of my memory can conjure up
> the faintest image of what that colour was. I try blue, and gold, and
> violet, and red, but none of them will fit . . . The other was its angle.
> It was not at right angles to the floor. But as soon as I have said this,
> I hasten to add that this way of putting it is a later reconstruction
> . . . The impression, however produced was that *this creature had*
> *reference to some horizontal, to some whole system of directions,*
> *based outside the earth, and that its mere presence imposed that*
> *alien system on me and abolished the terrestrial horizontal.* (Lewis,
> 1944, pp. 16–17, emphasis mine)

Lewis recognizes that there is an orientation to life, which we'll think of as
the Kingdom of God, that is correct by a set of standards we can't quite see.

Following Lewis' lead, we can see the Christian University as an outpost of the Kingdom of God. It operates on slightly different rules. In all
cases, our orientation isn't to some educational institution among thousands of educational institutions, but rather to provide a model of "how
things are supposed to be." Like Lewis' Eldil, there's a sense in which this
way of living in community feels strange but simultaneously right. The orientation comes from another way of living: one drawing from Kingdom
principles.

At the beginning of this book, I had Obi-Wan Kenobi explaining to
Luke Skywalker that he had entered a new world; the world of a Jedi knight.
In that regard, it made sense to think of your transition into college as entering a new world. While that is true, it's incomplete. If the Christian university is an embodiment of the Kingdom of God, an outpost of how things
are supposed to be, then it's a whole new world at a much deeper level
than leaving home. It's about participating in that world where Kingdom
principles become second nature.

This is why comparisons to state schools are unnecessary when defining the Christian university. Our motivation comes from a very different
place. We do what we do because we are together in building God's Kingdom, helping people grasp their unique calling, and pursuing an interdependence that looks like the Body of Christ. The *"Christian"* in Christian
university is at the heart of everything we do and cannot be reduced to
chapel, Bible classes, worship songs, and personal testimony.

I've talked about your college years as the Second Big Transition. It's
the point where you move out of your house of origin, relocate to new

place, and begin to explore life as an adult. It reflects a break from what you knew and counted on, what you took for granted. Now you have to think about a host of new things: perspectives, temptations, opportunities, and challenges. You build new friendships and find yourself stretched by them. You explore ideas you'd never carefully considered in classes and around the dining table.

But we're also concerned about the Third Big Transition. While it may have seemed like your high school years took forever, you college years will pass by very quickly. By the end of your first semester, you'll have a hard time remembering what it was like to be in high school. By your junior year in college, you won't remember what you thought as a freshman.

There's nothing wrong with that. You're on a journey. The good news is, like those on the road in the Wizard of Oz, you aren't alone. You have many others alongside you who are also trying to develop habits of living in the Kingdom of God.

Everything you are doing during your years in the Christian university is preparation for engagement in a complex, postmodern world. You will know who you are, whom you are following, and how to work with others to bring grace into the situations in which you find yourself.

Because you've gotten a glimpse of what the Kingdom of God can look like, you can recreate that anywhere you are. It will be different than your college years, because those around you may not "get" Kingdom principles. But your ability to be salt and light is immense, precisely because it's become second nature to you.

Educators like to talk about something called telos: the end goal of an activity. We looked early in this book at the reasons why you might pursue a Christian college education. You may be interested in a Christian environment or pursuit of a job or a degree or personal growth or all of the above. But the Christian university doesn't exist just for these reasons.

The Christian university exists to build God's Kingdom. Sometimes that means we challenge the powers that support human trafficking. Sometimes it means that we urge the evangelical church to address important changes in society. Sometimes it means we write and produce movies. Sometimes it means that we ensure that an accounting firm operates in ways that aren't just ethical but that support human flourishing.

You have taken the first step into a much larger world. It's the beginning of a tremendous adventure for you, for your faculty, for your administrators, for your coaches, for your family. But college isn't the end of the adventure any more than the Emerald City was the end of the Yellow Brick Road. It's but a relatively brief stop along the road of the bigger adventure that we all share. From here you will significantly change the world for God and his Kingdom.

Your story will be grafted into mine, into that of your classmates, into all those at the university. Ultimately, all stories get caught up in God's own story of re-creation.

We started this journey with the Apostle Peter having a vision on a balcony. It was a vision that he didn't expect but that he embraced, expanding the reach of the Kingdom. In the same way, I pray that we all have our eyes continually opened to the new things God wants to show us. For of such is the Kingdom of God.

Bibliography

Abraham, W. J. (2010). *Aldersgate and Athens: John Wesley and the Foundations of Christian Belief*. Waco, TX: Baylor University Press.

Adams, D. (1981). *The Hitchhiker's Guide to the Galaxy*. New York: Pocket Books.

Arnett, J. J. (2004). *Emerging Adulthood: The Winding Road from the Late Teens through the Twenties*. New York; Oxford: Oxford University Press.

Arum, R., & Roksa, J. (2011). *Academically Adrift: Limited Learning on College Campuses*. Chicago: University of Chicago Press.

Astin, A. W. (2000). How the Liberal Arts College Affects Students. In S. Koblick & S. R. Graubard (Eds.), *Distinctively American: The Residential Liberal Arts Colleges* (pp. 77–100). New Brunswick, NJ: Transaction.

Bain, K. (2004). *What the Best College Teachers Do*. Cambridge, MA: Harvard University Press.

———. (2012). *What the Best College Students Do*. Cambridge, MA: The Belknap Press of Harvard University Press.

Baron, R. A., Byrne, D., & Branscombe, N. R. (2007). *Mastering Social Psychology*. Boston: Allyn and Bacon.

Baum, L. F., & Denslow, W. W. (1900). *The Wonderful Wizard of Oz*. Chicago; New York: G.M. Hill Co.

Berger, K. S. (2011). *The Developing Person Through the Life Span*. New York, NY: Worth

Bethke, J. (2012). *"Why I hate religion but love Jesus."*

Bogle, K. A. (2008). *Hooking Up: Sex, Dating, and Relationships on Campus*. New York: New York University Press.

Bok, D. C. (2006). *Our Underachieving Colleges: A Candid Look at How Much Students Learn and Why They Should Be Learning More*. Princeton, NJ: Princeton University Press.

Bonhoeffer, D. (1954). *Life Together* (1st ed.). New York,: Harper.

Boyatzis, R. (2003). [personal e-mail].

Boyer, E. L., & Carnegie Foundation for the Advancement of Teaching. (1987). *College: The Undergraduate Experience in America* (1st ed.). New York: Harper & Row.

Bruggemann, W. (2010). *Journey to the Common Good*. Louisville, KY: Westminster John Knox Press.

Budde, M. L., & Wright, J. W. (2004). *Conflicting Allegiances: The Church-based University in a Liberal Democratic Society*. Grand Rapids, MI: Brazos Press.

Buechner, F. (1993). *Wishful Thinking: A Seeker's ABC (Revised and Expanded)*: Harper Collins.

Claerbaut, D. (2004). *Faith and Learning on the Edge: A Bold New Look at Religion in Higher Education*. Grand Rapids, MI: Zondervan.

Clifton, D. O., & Anderson, E. C. (2002). *StrengthsQuest: Discover and Develop Your Strengths in Academics, Career, and Beyond* (1st ed.). Washington, DC: Gallup Organization.

Cohn, D. V., Jeffrey Passel, Wendy Wang, Gretchen Livingston. (2011). "Barely Half of U.S. Adults Are Married—A Record Low." Retrieved June 27, 2012, from http://www.pewsocialtrends.org/2011/12/14/barely-half-of-u-s-adults-are-married-a-record-low/.

Collins, F. S. (2006). *The Language of God: A Scientist Presents Evidence for Belief*. New York: Free Press.

Davis, K. (2011). *Kisses From Katie: A Story of Relentless Love and Redemption*. New York, NY: Howard Books.

de Vise, D. (2012). "Is College Too Easy? As Study Time Falls, Debate Rises." Retrieved July 10, 2012, from http://www.washingtonpost.com/local/education/is-college-too-easy-as-study-time-falls-debate-rises/2012/05/21/gIQAp7uUgU_story.html.

Dean, K. C. (2010). *Almost Christian: What the Faith of Our Teenagers Is Telling the American Church*. Oxford; New York: Oxford University Press.

Dockery, D. S., & Thornbury, G. A. (2002). *Shaping a Christian Worldview: The Foundations of Christian Higher Education*. Nashville, TN: Broadman & Holman.

Dowdall, G. W. (2009). *College Drinking: Reframing a Social Problem*. Westport, CN: Praeger.

Evans, R. H. (2010). *Evolving in Monkey Town: How a Girl Who Knew All the Answer Learned to Ask Questions*. Grand Rapids, MI: Zondervan.

Fowler, J. W. (1981). *Stages of Faith: The Psychology of Human Development and the Quest for Meaning* (1st ed.). San Francisco: Harper & Row.

Gardner, H. (1993). *Multiple Intelligences: The Theory in Practice*. New York: Basic Books.

Goleman, D., Boyatzis, R., & McKee, A. (2002). *Primal Leadership: Realizing the Power of Emotional Intelligence*. Boston, MA: Harvard Business School Press.

Herek, S. (Writer). (1992). *The Mighty Ducks*: Disney.

Hersh, R. H. (2000). "Generating Ideals and Transforming LIves: A Contemporary Case for the Residential Liberal Arts College." In S. a. G. Koblick, Stephen R. (eds) (Ed.), *Distinctively American: The Residential Liberal Arts College* (pp. 173–94). New Brunswick, NJ: Transaction Publishing.

Holmes, A. F. (1975). *The Idea of a Christian College*. Grand Rapids, MI: W. B. Eerdmans.

Hughes, R. T. (2001). *How Christian Faith Can Sustain the Life of the Mind*. Grand Rapids, MI: Wm. B. Eerdmans.

Hunter, J. D. (1983). *American Evangelicalism: Conservative Religion and the Quandary of Modernity*. New Brunswick, NJ: Rutgers University Press.

———. (2010). *To Change the World: The Irony, Tragedy, and Possibility of Christianity in the Late Modern World*. New York: Oxford University Press.

Jacobsen, D. G., Jacobsen, R. H., & Sawatsky, R. (2004). *Scholarship and Christian Faith: Enlarging the Conversation*. Oxford; New York: Oxford University Press.

Julian, T., & Kiminski, R. (2011). Education and Synthetic Work-Life Earnings Estimates Retrieved July 6, 2012, from http://www.census.gov/prod/2011pubs/acs-14.pdf.

Keeling, R. P., & Hersh, R. H. (2011). *We're Losing Our Minds: Rethinking American Higher Education* (1st ed.). New York: Palgrave Macmillan.

Kelley, D. M. (1972). *Why Conservative Churches Are Growing: A Study in Sociology of Religion* (1st ed.). New York: Harper & Row.

Kinnaman, D., & Hawkins, A. (2011). *You Lost Me: Why Young Christians Are Leaving Church—and Rethinking Faith*. Grand Rapids, MI: BakerBooks.

Kinnaman, D., & Lyons, G. (2007). *Unchristian: What a New Generation Really Thinks about Christianity—and Why It Matters*. Grand Rapids, MI: Baker Books.

Langley, N., Ryerson, F. & Woolf, E., writers. (1939). *The Wizard of Oz*. Warner Bros.

Larson, E. J. (1997). *Summer for the Gods: The Scopes Trial and America's Continuing Debate over Science and Religion*. New York: BasicBooks.

Lewis, C. S. (1944). *Perelandra*. New York, NY: Scribner.

Litfin, A. D. (2004). *Conceiving the Christian College*. Grand Rapids, MI: W. B. Eerdmans Pub. Co.

Lyons-Pardue, K. J., & Sturdevant, J. (2011). "Reading the Bible in a Postmodern Age: The Importance of Context for Interpretation." In R. P. Thompson & T. J. Oord (Eds.), *The Bible Tells Me So: Reading the Bible as Scripture* (pp. 141–16). Nampa, ID: SacraSage.

Maddox, R. L. (1994). *Responsible Grace: John Wesley's Practical Theology*. Nashville, TN: Kingswood Books.

Manning, B. (2010). *All Is Grace: A Ragamuffin Memoir*. Colorado Springs, CO: David C. Cook.

McKnight, S. (2011). *The King Jesus Gospel: The Original Good News Revisited*. Grand Rapids, MI: Zondervan.

McNeal, R. (2003). *The Present Future: Six Tough Questions for the Church*. San Francisco, CA: John Wiley and Sons.

Menand, L. (2010). *The Marketplace of Ideas* (1st ed.). New York: W. W. Norton.

Miles, R. L. (1997). "The Instrumental Role of Reason." In W. S. Gunter, S. J. Jones, T. A. Campbell, R. L. Miles & R. L. Maddox (Eds.), *Wesley and the Quadrilateral: Renewing the Conversation*. Nashville, TN: Abingdon.

Oord, T. J. (2009). "Types of Postmodernism." In J. R. Akkerman, T. J. Oord & B. Peterson (Eds.), *Postmodern and Wesleyan? Exploring the Boundaries and Possibilities*. Kansas City, MO: Beacon Hill Press.

———. (2010). "Reclaiming the Past / Imagining a Future: Revisionary Postmodernism." Retrieved from http://thomasjayoord.com/index.php/blog/archives/reclaiming_to_move_ahead_revisionary_postmodernism/ - .UiSZKmTwJgI.

Palmer, P. J. (1993). *To Know as We Are Known: Education as a Spiritual Journey* (1st HarperCollins pbk ed.). San Francisco: HarperSanFrancisco.

———. (1998). *The Courage to Teach: Exploring the Inner Landscape of a Teacher's Life* (1st ed.). San Francisco, CA: Jossey-Bass.

———. (2000). *Let Your Life Speak: Listening for the Voice of Vocation*. San Francisco: Jossey-Bass.

———. (2004). *A Hidden Wholeness: The Journey toward an Undivided Life—Welcoming the Soul and Weaving Community in a Wounded World*. San Francisco, CA: Jossey-Bass.

Parks, S. D. (2000). *Big Questions, Worthy Dreams: Mentoring Young Adults in Their Serach for Meaning, Purpose, and Faith*. San Francisco, CA: Jossey-Bass.

Pascarella, E. T., Bohr, L., Nora, A., & Terenzini, P. T. (1995). "Intercollegiate Athletic Participation and Freshman-Year Cognitive Outcomes." *The Journal of Higher Education, 66*(4), 369–87. doi: 10.2307/2943793.

Bibliography

Peck, M. S. (1978). *The Road Less Traveled: A New Psychology of Love, Traditional Values, and Spiritual Growth*. New York: Simon and Schuster.

———. (1987). *The Different Drum: Community-Making and Peace*. New York: Simon and Schuster.

———. (1993). *A World Waiting to Be Born: Civility Rediscovered*. New York: Bantam Books.

Postman, N. (1995). *The End of Education: Redefining the Value of School* (1st ed.). New York: Knopf.

Pryor, J. H., DeAngelo, L., Blake, L. P., Hurtado, S., & Tran, S. (2011). "The American Freshman: National Norms 2011." Retrieved July 6, 2012, from http://heri.ucla.edu/PDFs/pubs/TFS/Norms/Monographs/TheAmericanFreshman2011.pdf.

Putnam, R. D. (2000). *Bowling Alone: The Collapse and Revival of American Community*. New York: Simon & Schuster.

Putnam, R. D., & Campbell, D. E. (2010). *American Grace: How Religion Divides and Unites Us* (1st Simon & Schuster hardcover ed.). New York: Simon & Schuster.

Rojstaczer, S., & Healy, C. (2012). "Where A Is Ordinary: The Evolution of American College and University Grading, 1940–2009." Retrieved July 9, 2012, from http://www.tcrecord.org ID Number: 16473.

Ross, G. (Writer). (2012). *The Hunger Games*: Lions Gate.

Runyon, T. (1998). *The New Creation: John Wesley's Theology Today*. Nashville, TN: Abingdon.

Smith, C. (2009). *Souls in Transition: The Religious and Spiritual Lives of Emerging Adults*. Oxford: Oxford University Press.

Smith, C., Christoffersen, K. M., Davidson, H., & Herzog, P. S. (2011). *Lost in Transition: The Dark Side of Emerging Adulthood*. New York: Oxford University Press.

Smith, C., & Denton, M. L. (2005). *Soul Searching: The Religious and Spiritual Lives of American Teenagers*. Oxford ; New York: Oxford University Press.

Smith, J. K. A. (2009). *Desiring the Kingdom: Worship, Worldview, and Cultural Formation*. Grand Rapids, MI: Baker Academic.

Snyder, H. A. (1980). *The Radical Wesley and Patterns for Church Renewal*. Downer's Grove, IL: InterVarsity Press.

———. (2011). *Yes in Christ: Wesleyan Reflections on Gospel, Mission, and Culture*. Toronto: Clements Academic.

Taylor, D. (1996). *The Healing Power of Stories: Creating Yourself through the Stories of Your Life* (1st ed.). New York: Doubleday.

Thompson, D. (2012). "Where Did All the Workers Go? 60 Years of Economic Change in 1 Graph." Retrieved July 6, 2012, from http://www.theatlantic.com/business/archive/2012/01/where-did-all-the-workers-go-60-years-of-economic-change-in-1-graph/252018/.

Tomkins, S. (2003). *John Wesley: A Biography*. Grand Rapids, MI: Wm. B. Eerdmans Pub. Co.

Troop, D. (2011). "The Beloit College Mind-Set List Welcomes the 'Internet Class,'" from http://chronicle.com/article/The-Beloit-College-Mind-Set/128783/.

Vander Ven, T. (2011). *Getting Wasted: Why College Students Drink Too Much and Party So Hard*. New York: New York University Press.

Vickers, J. E. (2010). "Wesley's Theological Emphases." In R. L. Maddox & J. E. Vickers (Eds.), *Cambridge Companions to John Wesley* (pp. xi, 342 p.). Cambridge ; New York: Cambridge University Press.

Warren, R. (2002). *The Purpose-Driven Life: What on Earth Am I Here For?* Grand Rapids, MI: Zondervan.

Wesley, J. (1746). "The Means of Grace." Retrieved August 6, 2012, from http://wesley. nnu.edu/john-wesley/the-sermons-of-john-wesley-1872-edition/sermon-16-the-means-of-grace/.

Wolfe, T. (2004). *I Am Charlotte Simmons*. New York: Picador Press.

Wright, N. T. (2010). *After You Believe: Why Christian Character Matters* (1st ed.). New York, NY: HarperOne.

———. (2012). *How God Became King: The Forgotten Story of the Gospels* (1st. ed.). New York: HarperOne.

Made in the USA
Columbia, SC
22 August 2017